THE MISADVENTURES OF
# AWKWARD
## BLACK GIRL

# THE MISADVENTURES OF
# AWKWARD
# BLACK GIRL

## Issa Rae

**37 INK**

—

**ATRIA**

New York   London   Toronto   Sydney   New Delhi

**ATRIA** BOOKS          37INK

A Division of Simon & Schuster, Inc.
1230 Avenue of the Americas
New York, NY 10020

First 37 Ink/Atria Books hardcover edition February 2015

**37 INK** / **ATRIA** BOOKS and colophon are trademarks of Simon & Schuster, Inc.

For information about special discounts for bulk purchases, please contact Simon & Schuster Special Sales at 1-866-506-1949 or business@simonandschuster.com.

The Simon & Schuster Speakers Bureau can bring authors to your live event. For more information or to book an event, contact the Simon & Schuster Speakers Bureau at 1-866-248-3049 or visit our website at www.simonspeakers.com.

Interior design by Meryll Rae Preposi

Manufactured in the United States of America

10   9   8   7   6   5   4   3   2   1

Library of Congress Cataloging-in-Publication Data is available.

ISBN 978-1-4767-4905-1
ISBN 978-1-4767-4909-9 (ebook)

*To Mom, Dad, Amadou, Malick, Lamine,
Elize, Memée, and Papa.*

# Contents

# THE MISADVENTURES OF
# AWKWARD
# BLACK GIRL

# Introduction

My name is Jo-Issa Rae Diop and I've always wanted a nickname. For the first twelve years of my life, none of my friends were lazy enough to shorten the pronunciation of my name, or affectionately bold enough to replace my name with an entirely new word, like Cocoa or Jollyrancher. Because every cool person I knew had a nickname, I decided not to wait on anyone to do me the honor. So in the fourth grade, when a substitute teacher came to take the place of Ms. Osei, I took the opportunity to publicly anoint myself with a new lovable identity. I waited as the teacher called roll, for once excited about the impending mispronunciation (if it wasn't my first name, it was *always* my last name). She couldn't get to the Ds fast enough. This time, I'd not only correct her, but I'd intervene with a name that was both easy to pronounce and fun and adventurous, just like me.

"Joe-EYE-suh . . . uh, DIE-OP?" she asked, pretending to look through the sea of white kids to find my ethnic ass.

"Here! It's Jo-EEE-SUH JOPE, but my friends call me . . .

Sloppy Jo." I chuckled as I looked around the class, waiting for the high-fives and acknowledgment from my classmates that never came. All that accompanied my announcement *was* my own laugh, and two seconds of silence as the teacher looked at me and nodded, processing the ridiculousness of my suggestion.

"Right. Jo-E-SUH," the sub continued. "Sarah Dotson?"

"Here," Sarah said.

Hot with regret at my blatant attempt to rebrand myself, I sat, defeated, as the teacher continued down the sheet of names. I had conceived my new nickname the previous Friday, after a delicious school lunch. One part self-depreciative humor and one part clever wordplay, the name seemed perfect. Now that nobody had so much as looked in my direction after my made-up proclamation, I just felt silly. *Who wants to be "sloppy" anyway?* That teacher probably saved herself from a lawsuit. Can you imagine calling the sole black girl in the class "sloppy"? Good for her indifference. I'm thankful for it. What an absolutely stupid and embarrassing nickname from a painfully childish mind. (If I could go back in time and slap all of the idiocy out of my mouth, I would be a busy time traveler.)

Where my first name has been an individual struggle, my last name has, appropriately, been a family battle. Having spent some of my youth in Senegal or around Senegalese people in America, I never could have imagined that my monosyllabic family name would have so many alternate, incorrect variations. There's "DIE-OP," "DEE-OP," "DIP," "JIP," "JOP," and my personal favorite, "DEE-POH."

In high school, I found no burden in correcting people. It wasn't their fault that they didn't know, and there was no harm done. My annoyance would emerge when people would take it upon themselves to correct me in the pronunciation of my *own name*! It would go something like this:

"DEE-OP?"

"Oh, it's pronounced 'Jope,' as in 'rhymes with hope,' " I would say with a smile.

"But . . . it's *spelled* D-I-O-P. 'Dee-op,' " they would say with confused indignation.

"Yeah, I know. It's still 'JOPE.' "

"Oh . . . kay," they'd hesitantly resign.

This happened way more frequently than it should have, and I couldn't for the life of me figure out why. Until one person I went back and forth with for far too long maintained that her doctor's last name was the same as mine and he pronounced it "DEE-OP." I rolled my eyes. "Just forget it," I would have said, except her doctor was none other than my father. What the heck, Dad? Family pride, much?

My dad is a mini-celebrity in South Central, on account that his Inglewood clinic has his name in big white letters on the rectangular brick building that lines Manchester Boulevard, one of the major streets in the area (my high school bus actually passed the building on its route). I went to high school in South Central, on the border of Compton and Watts, where many of my classmates claimed my father as their childhood pediatrician.

"Oh, are you related to Dr. Dee-Op on Manchester?"

"Dr. Diop? Yeah."

"No, Dr. Dee-Op."

"It's Diop. And yeah."

"Oh . . . kay . . . *If you say so . . .*"

I confronted my dad about this one day after school.

"Dad, why are you telling people our last name is Dee-Op?"

"Because they'll mess it up anyway," he said with a shrug.

"But you have to correct them!"

"I got tired of correcting them," he calmly retorted.

I shook my head. How could I properly defend my name if the man with the accent himself wouldn't co-sign it?

I did eventually get that nickname I so yearned for, though it came much later, in my early twenties. I was wall-to-wall chatting on Facebook with Kisha, one of my good friends from college. After four years of friendship, she randomly decided to address me as "Issa Rae" with no warning whatsoever. After my dear Aunt Rae passed in January of 2008, I had changed my name on Facebook from "Jo-Issa Diop" to include my middle name, Rae, in her honor. Kisha had no idea she had given me both a new way to honor the memory of my aunt and an alter ego for my creative endeavors, though I didn't realize it until I was brainstorming names for my blog and the name Issa Rae flashed before me. Initially, I wanted a clever name, like "JoDi" (a rap alias I used with my younger brother) or "FloJo, the Filmmaker." But I also needed a name that could house all of my creative work, films included. Issa Rae as an alias was just the thing, as it was way cooler than Jo-IssaRaeDiop.com and would protect me, in case I ever needed to get a "real" job. All the trash I talked online would be traced back to Issa Rae and the HR departments would be none the wiser. Plus, the name "Issa," though still easy to mispronounce, was way more visually digestible than "Jo-Issa."

All this to say, in this book, you'll see my government name referenced a lot. I only started referring to myself as Issa Rae in 2008, and so all stories prior to that will reference my birth name. Deal with it.

Here's something else you'll have to deal with: My family moved around a lot and I switched schools every two years until high school, so don't even bother trying to keep up; I don't blame you for your confusion. Just know that each school switch represented a new opportunity for me to try, again, to be less awkward, to be a little bit cooler, to be a little bit smarter and wiser. "Try" being the operative word.

As for the stories, I'm coming clean with all the awkward, the embarrassing, the disappointing, the frustrating moments that have made me me, many of which have turned out to be teaching moments—which is why I occasionally throw in an ABG Guide for awkward situations in which you might find yourself, such as "Public Grazing," an aid to eating in front of people, or "When Co-workers Attack."

Whether you're an awkward black girl or a confident white guy, my hope is that you'll learn from my mistakes and, at the very least, laugh at my misgivings.

Awkwardly yours,

### Issa Rae

# AISIL

At only eleven years of age, I was a cyber ho. Looking back, I'm embarrassed. For me. For my parents. But oddly enough, my cyber social debauchery is indirectly correlated with my current status as a so-called internet pioneer. It all started when I began catfishing—creating characters and transmitting them over the internet—though back then people just called it "lying." Had my father not signed my entire family up with America Online accounts for the computer in our modest Potomac, Maryland, home I don't know that I'd have had the tools to exploit the early ages of the internet.

Two years earlier, my oldest brother, Amadou, had gone away to college at Morehouse, freeing up the coveted computer, which was housed in the basement, for my use. Before he decamped for college, I would spend hours at a time watching him type the commands into MS-DOS that would transport us to the magical kingdom of Sierra's *King's Quest VI* on our IBM. I never had a strong desire to play the game myself—I always assumed I wasn't smart enough to play it on my own—until Amadou graduated from the house and I no longer had anyone to excitedly observe. I looked up to my oldest brother as the epitome of intelligence. He knew *everything*, though he was too humble to be ostentatious with his knowledge as I would have been had I been as smart. So I simply observed. At eighteen, he was an official adult, and he had a duty to selflessly spread his intelligence to the world, other people's younger sisters included. His absence left a void in my heart and in the basement, particularly where the use of the computer was concerned.

I wasn't next in line for the computer, but my second-oldest brother, Malick, was too preoccupied with football, girls, and high school to care. He'd occasionally make use of it for term papers and Tetris, but otherwise, it was mine for the taking. Using the computer wasn't foreign to me, by any means. I had an old Apple computer in my very own room (a double source of jealousy for my younger brother), where I played *Number Munchers* and self-published my stories on perforated paper from an excruciatingly noisy printer.

"Jo-Issa, are you wasting paper again?!" my mother would yell from her makeshift home office, tipped off by the mechanical snitch. When alone, and mom-approved, I actually loved to hear the robotic crunching and whirring that the printer made while laying to ink my very own written words. But the computer in my room paled in comparison to the one downstairs, in the basement. For one thing, the large floppy disks—I think they were actually called hard disks, what the *f%4# 90s?*—were becoming extinct, and rightfully so, since the data on those things could be lost with the smudge of a finger. And since my computer took only the "hard" disks, my game choices were limited to nerdy learning games and text-based adventure games with no visuals. BLECH. BORING. BOO.

The other reason my computer wasn't a huge triumph for my

preteen self-discovery was because it lacked a modem, which meant no dial-up internet for me. But AOL changed my life. Specifically, it changed my social life. To be more precise: AOL *gave* me a social life. It ignited my social development and expanded my concept of sexuality. Because of AOL, I had imaginary friends that weren't imaginary. I had elaborate conversations devoid of awkward silences. And, perhaps most valuable of all, I could actually talk to boys. At my command!

Before my parents caught wind of frightening news reports of child predators, I spent my days and after-school evenings in chat rooms, learning to speed read, talking to kids my age who were also ahead of the curve. Or pedophiles, who were remarkably creative and persistent in their forbidden pursuit. Pedos actually had it *made* in the mid-nineties, before the media exposed them. Talk about the glory days.

My friends at school, other fifth graders, didn't seem to relate when I mentioned "chat rooms" and "profiles" or when I sang along to the dial-up internet song I made up in my head. It seemed that, for a brief moment, only I was privy to this alternate American universe that lived online.

By the time my family moved to Los Angeles to join my dad, a pediatrician, who had seized an opportunity to open his own family clinic there, my relationship with the computer had grown immensely, much to the dismay and irritation of my mother.

"You're always on the computer! Go do your homework."

"I already finished."

"Well then, go outside and play!"

She just didn't get it. Only recently, in my late twenties, did she come to realize that my excessive computer use is what led me to becoming the self-employed, almost-focused career woman I am today.

By the summer of 1996, more of my friends from Maryland had adopted AOL. It helped us bridge the three thousand miles between us. By then, I was already over the handwritten letters of yesteryear. That was a form of communication of the third world, reserved for pen pals from Ghana and Spain. Besides, the "You've Got Mail" greeting was *way* more exciting than the dead silence of receiving a letter. Exclaiming, "I've got mail!" in the foyer to yourself isn't the same—trust me.

It was through electronic mail that I'd tell my friends back home about my Hollywood adventures. Never mind the fact that I lived in Windsor Hills, thirty minutes away from Hollywood, and that I was struggling to make friends. Or that my sense of style was horrendous, and my middle school had done away with lockers so the authorities could better monitor drug use. ALL I EVER WANTED WAS A LOCKER! I felt robbed of the middle school experience I saw on *Boy Meets World* and *Doug*, but my friends didn't have to know that. I led them to believe I was on the brink of stardom, just by breathing in the recycled smog of other celebrities around me. Plus, I lived down the street from Ray Charles's old house. I was famous by association.

Our move back to Los Angeles also fulfilled a dream I'd held on to for five whole years: we were finally reunited with my father. He'd visit us in Maryland once every two to three months for an extended period of time, but for the most part, I spent my elementary school years without him and, in his absence, had constructed a superheroic, Arnold Schwarzenegger-esque Father of the Year image of him in my mind. My dad was *the* man, and whenever I'd tell my teachers my father was a doctor who was too busy to come to Back to School night, their surprised and delighted "Oh!" always gave me a sense of pride. I didn't speculate then that they were making an assumption about my family's income and placing my blackness into a Huxtable category. To me, their reaction implied that a doctor was an important profession, which meant my dad was important. And I wanted to be just like my dad.

I so longed to live with him and see my family complete, I neglected to figure out that the reunion meant double supervision. The only computer in the house was in my dad's home office, and now internet activity was being monitored without my knowing it. Going through puberty during the dawn of the internet could have left me unscathed if my dad weren't so annoyingly tech savvy. If only he, a native African, were like the tribal stereotypes I read about in my middle school history books, I would have gotten away with so much more. Instead, I found myself sneaking to look up "sex" in the encyclopedia and then cross-referencing my findings with the Yahoo.com search results. Also, unbeknownst to me, my dad had added a kid-safe image blocker, so I was always limited to boring text-only definitions.

I was wrought with hormones and obsessed with finding a boyfriend. All I knew was that boys cared about sex and I didn't know enough about it. I was too embarrassed to ask my peers. They were already über-judgmental about my naïveté to all things black after I accidentally exposed myself when Tupac died. "Two-pack died? What did he sing?"

Normally, I would have been spared from middle school humiliation by asking my two older brothers directly. They would have happily explained who Tupac was and I would have happily plagiarized their responses and relayed their feelings about him as my own. But my second-oldest brother had by then also graduated from the house to go to college and I was left as the oldest in the house. If I had trouble attracting the boys at my school before, my ignorance about Tupac destroyed any remote chance I might have had.

All I knew was that I had all these developing feelings for boys and that I wanted desperately for them to notice me. They did, but for reasons that didn't help my quest: my nap-tural hair; my underdeveloped, seemingly concave breasts; my white-girl accent, and my tomboyish appearance. The prototype of lust for the boys my age was a light-skinned girl with long hair, and I just didn't fit that profile. But I didn't want to believe that. So I would imagine instead that I held the interest of all the boys and often convinced myself of that. All the while, I remained the continued object of disdain from my peers. I often found myself emboldened whenever a guy would show me any attention at all, i.e. "Ay, you did the homework? Let me copy," or "You got ten cents for the vending machine?" I blame any misread social cues on *Saved by the Bell*. Zack and Kelly's romance was something I wanted so badly to emulate.

My first-ever junior high school dance was approaching and, with the help of a Saturday morning marathon of *Saved*, I built up the courage that Monday morning to talk to Remington, an eighth-grade-looking sixth-grader who I'm pretty sure had been held back (though nobody talked about it). He had thick facial hair and muscular, athletic arms. He *loved* women, and frequently expressed his sexual desires in a way that hinted at experience. In my eyes, he was the answer. And I had so many questions. One of them, I worked up the courage to ask in front of his friends. I approached him right after our Environmental Studies class was dismissed, casually, waiting for him to pick up his only school supply, a single folder.

"Hey, Remington," I started, shyly. "Are you going to the dance?"

He didn't miss a beat: "Not with you!"

His friends didn't even try to hide their laughter. Not a single one. I smiled and tried to play it off.

"Oh. No—I didn't mean that. You thought I was asking for me?"

But it was too late; they had already pushed past to leave me in the classroom alone, my Environmental Studies teacher avoiding eye contact with me.

Ever optimistic, I went to the dance by myself, with the hope that maybe a boy there would ask me to dance. Maybe it would be Quentin, the skinny, half-albino/half-effeminate boy to whom I'd been sending "secret admirer" letters. It was the least he could do, after excitedly exposing to the class that I had been writing him love notes for weeks. Despite my humiliation, I couldn't really blame him. It happened naturally enough. The homeroom teacher brought up "secret admirers" in her announcement about Valentine's Day grams.

"Does anyone know what a 'secret admirer' is?" she asked.

"I do! I do, Ms. Nash!"

My heart plummeted to my stomach as I noticed him anxiously looking in my direction.

"What do you know about secret admirers, Quentin?" asked Ms. Nash.

"That girl right there was writing me 'secret admirer' notes." He smiled at me, as if his public acknowledgment didn't violate the very purpose of the "secret" in "secret admirer."

Surely, he would save me from walking around the junior high dance all alone, in the jean jumper and white turtleneck I had packed in my backpack just for this after-school occasion. (I never wore dresses.) Somebody had to take notice and ask me to dance, based on that alone. Unfortunately, no one ever asked.

I was rapidly coming to the conclusion that boys didn't find me attractive. That was heartbreaking. My self-esteem was in danger and had it not been for the saving grace of the Instant Message feature on AOL, I probably would have suffered death by trying too hard.

I don't remember the first time I typed to a stranger. It wasn't monumental for me. But it did speak to a desire to escape myself. For one thing, I could be anyone I wanted to be online. With each swift keystroke, a new, fearless identity emerged. I could be light-skinned with long hair, or blue-eyed with blond hair. Or experienced, witty, and seductive—things nobody saw me as in real life. I could be *anyone's* type and was able to do so because during the early stages of AOL, pictures were pretty rare, though around the time that IMs came along, home scanners were growing more popular. Thankfully, however, pictures took forever to upload and weren't in high demand, so people were content with self-descriptions. As people tended to be quite generous in their descriptions of themselves, I figured I could be, too. What did it matter?

"A/S/L," the pop-up conversation would start.

Age/Sex/Location? (This blatant acronym *had* to have been tooled by pedophiles. The genius!) There was something flattering about being selected out of a pool of thirty to sixty people in a chat room for a private talk. I'd imagine it was like being chosen at a party to dance, though I wouldn't know anything about that. But for my chameleon-esque purposes, responding to this conversation opener was the hardest part. I couldn't become a type if I didn't know what I was working with. If I were in the mood to talk to someone my age, I'd be honest.

*"11/F/Cali, u?"*
*"13/f/aʒ. hi."*

*Trick, I don't want no friends right now!* On to the next. Sometimes I'd be the pursuer. I'd visit the *R&B*, *Rap*, or *Games* chat rooms and scout screen names that would give me hints at my preferred types: soccrplaya83, muscleman39, blkboy17. All I had were snippets of open chats to go by. What were they contributing to the larger public conversation? I couldn't choose someone who was *too* active in the chat room; his chances of committing to a one-on-one were slim. Besides, someone who revels in being the center of attention is not my type. I don't like to compete. Instead, I went for those who would contribute a few meaningful phrases here and there: "games are cool" or "yah i love r. kelly." Subtle hints like those were enough to provoke me to reach out.

I'd begin:

SuGaLuv112: *"hi. a/s/l?"*
MUSCLEMAN39: *"18/m/de. u??"*
SuGaLuv112: *"17/f/cali."*
MUSCLEMAN39: *"cool, what's up?"*
SuGaLuv112: *"nothin. chillin. bored."*
MUSCLEMAN39: *"are you horny?"*

*What? Like rhinos?* My knowledge of internet slang was coming up empty. But I tried.

SuGaLuv112: *"what do u you mean?"*

Then came the door-slam sound effect from my computer speakers.

MUSCLEMAN39 HAS SIGNED OFF.

After a couple of weeks, and some more of these incidents, I decided to finally look up the definition of "horny." What was being asked of me? My Encarta CD-ROM produced no answers, but Yahoo was full of them.

hor-ny (hôr nē): desiring of sexual activity.

*Oh my freaking God. Of course. YES!* That's exactly what I was. The answer to what I was looking for in so many ways was being dangled before me, and all I had to do was respond with a simple "yes." I couldn't wait for the next opportunity to showcase my new personality trait. I sought it, thirstily. This time ready for the exchange and wealth of knowledge that would follow. I was so appropriately excited and ready.

My first online relationship started off innocently enough. Every day after school, around three thirty, I would log on. It was the perfect time. My mom, who was too tired to worry about her remaining three kids, after dealing with one hundred plus of her French students, would go take a nap. During that time, *nobody* could go in and disturb her. Unless there was a fire, or an intruder—Jehovah's Witnesses didn't count—we had all learned by swift-slap punishment that we were to respect her nap time. It was the one time slot of the day—thirty minutes or sometimes a whole hour—that our adult supervision was lenient. Occasionally, I would play bossy and order my siblings around on behalf of my mother, but for the most part, I left them alone to focus on my own debauchery and thus began my first real online relationship.

He was nineteen; I had turned twelve. My parents were seven years apart, so . . . I guess it was cool? He described himself as white, athletically built, bald, with a red beard. When I first saw *American*

*History X* years later, in high school, I had a flash memory of him, as if I'd met him in a previous life. He was "pretty average looking" by his description, but by my imagination, he was beautiful. He was sensitive. He asked me—Jennifer was my white-girl name (same number of syllables as Jo-Issa)—about my day, about how I was doing. He expressed his feelings for me. Told me he felt stupid for thinking about me all the time when we'd never met. To him, I was blond-haired, blue-eyed, and petite. Technically, I *was* petite for an adult person, but definitely oversized for a sixth-grader.

Our conversations started out pretty casually at first, but they escalated quickly. And then he made the first move.

REDBEARD19: *what are you wearing?*
SuGaLuv112: *a tank top and shorts*

By then, I knew how to play the game. I had been asked the question via IM multiple times enough to know that a T-shirt, baggy jeans, and sneakers wasn't sexy enough. With redbeard19, I was slightly seasoned, and he only helped me to get better. He taught me so much about what ideal sex was supposed to be, what I could expect from future relationships. This was the prelude to sexting. The crazy part is, nothing about this turned me on. It was a learning experience for me. I would type what guys wanted to hear, while reading Spider-Man comic books or as *Tiny Toon Adventures* played in the background, satisfied that, while most of my peers were still virgins, at age twelve, I was mastering the art of cybersex.

After that first time, I started to feel a sense of guilt. In the classroom, I was anxious, worried that eyes were on me. I started to wonder if what I did was wrong. What would my teachers think if they knew? My parents? Could people tell? Did I look different?

One day in the spring, I sat in Ms. Frank's English class, unusually quiet. The teacher's pet, I owned this class. She reminded the class of that often, which only escalated their hatred of me. But that day, sick and in pain, I just didn't feel well. It was as if the butterflies inside my stomach had turned into dark moths, with razor-sharp antennas that were poking my sides and my midsection. I felt nauseous and dizzy. What was happening to me? I hadn't even had real sex!

Ms. Frank excused me to the nurse's office and I clutched my stomach and my throbbing head, worried about my pending diagnosis. I stopped at the restroom first to see if maybe I was experiencing a case of lunch food poisoning. And in that bathroom stall I discovered that, just like "Sally" in the Sex-Ed section of the Health textbook we had studied that winter, my body had begun to succumb to its transition to womanhood. Or as I thought at the time, *Ew gross, my vag is bleeding.*

I told the nurse I'd just gotten my period and she was super sympathetic, asking me if I wanted to go home. I did. I called my mother, who was transitioning into her new role as a stay-at-home mom and whispered my news into the phone.

"Mom, I got my pe . . ."

"What? Are you at school?"

"I don't feel good."

"What's wrong with you?"

"I got my period."

"Aww. My schubalubbalubba. I'm coming."

During the car ride home, as my mom snuck peeks at me and patted my leg for comfort, I wondered if I were being punished for my "fast" behavior. In Health class, we learned that a girl's period typically came around the time she was a teenager. I had just turned twelve. I was in a rush to grow up, but I didn't know if I wanted to be "grown" yet. I didn't want to be a woman, because that meant more responsibilities and expectations, and I was way too lazy for responsibilities and expectations. But then, my mom assuaged my worries with a simple declaration that changed everything for me.

"Guess you're a teenager now."

To hell with being a woman, I was a *teenager*. Teenagers like the kids on *90210* and *Saved by the Bell*. Finally! That was the missing link of my identity, and this bloody punctuation served as a head start to my new identity. I was a horny teenager.

My relationship with redbeard19 progressed as scanners became more readily available and he sent me a picture. He was nervous to do so, but he felt like I should see him. I was so excited. But also nervous. By then, I'd had several online flings here and there, but he was the only one with whom I had something "real." Also up until then, his face was an open canvas. It could change depending on what he said, or my mood. He wasn't a fully real person to me, with real feelings and real desires. He could have been lying to me in the same way that I was lying to him. We both could have had *Tiny Toons* on our television screens, scrambling to come up with novel sex words to stimulate each other. But the picture he sent demonstrated to me two things: 1) he was pretty damn honest—he appeared just as he said he would, and 2) he was actually kind of cute.

Something about our relationship wasn't the same after that. I felt like a fraud, and I was kind of turned off by how vulnerable he'd made himself. I stopped becoming available to him at the same time every day. I'd block him whenever I felt like prowling for new people to talk to, then unblock him when I was bored. He grew hurt and needy, and I grew disgusted and cold.

REDBEARD19: *what are you wearing today, baby?*

SuGaLuv112: *clothes.*

REDBEARD19: *take them off.*

[*5 minutes later*]

REDBEARD19: *u still there?*

SuGaLuv112: *sorry, was on the phone.*

REDBEARD19: *you don't have time for me anymore*

SuGaLuv112 HAS SIGNED OFF.

After that, I kept him blocked. By now, I was becoming a pro. Some kids had after-school sports, some had piano lessons, but "cybering" was now my after-school activity of choice. And for the most part, it felt safe. I wasn't "doing it" for real, so I was still pure. My actions were justified because I could still wear white for my future wedding (which, as with Zack and Kelly, would probably happen in college).

Now, pictures became a priority for me. If you didn't have a picture, I wasn't interested. As the most beautiful and sexy girl on the internet, I had a right to be picky. Not too much later, I met the guy of my dreams online. He sent me his picture after we got into a casual conversation about music. He was twenty-two, Italian, and black. He was one of the finest guys I had ever seen in my *life*, much less online. And he had multiple pictures of himself, so I knew it was real. Or was it? Thinking back, he sent me some very polished pictures—very modelesque. But whatever—he was real to me. I know he was real because he said he was Italian and black. And when we spoke on the phone, for the first time, he sounded like he was Italian and black; a Luigi-and-Tyrone hybrid, if you will.

His voice was so freaking sexy, though. I can't recall what

we would have talked about, what kind of engaging conversation starters came out of my twelve-year-old mouth. I just remember wondering why such a hottie like him was looking for people to talk to online. He seemed like the kind of guy who people would go out of their way to talk to. Just when I began to convince myself that this hot guy was courting me for me, he started pressing me for a picture. *Shit*. I had insisted that I didn't have a scanner in the past, but in an effort to keep him around, so he wouldn't get bored with me, I told him I planned to get one, just for him. So began the search. I'd have to do my best to find a picture that matched the description I gave him. He already thought I was eighteen. He thought I was African-American and light-skinned with long hair. So, thankfully, those nonspecifics gave me lots of options.

I don't remember where or how I found the picture—but she was gorgeous. She was who I wished I looked like. She looked like she could have been mixed race. My middle school peers would be all over her. In fact, I'm pretty sure I printed her picture out and told all the guys she was my cousin. "*That's* your cousin?! What side of the family? Where does she live?"

I sent him the picture, holding my breath. Would he believe me? Boy, did he! He was awestruck and excited, as if he'd hit the online jackpot. His interest in me grew: What did I do? Did I model? Was I dating? It felt amazing to be so beautiful. I envied the life of the real girl whose picture I stole. Did she know how lucky she had it? How easy her life was because she was so beautiful? And then the Blatalian wanted more. Maybe he was suspicious. Maybe he, too, felt like it was too good to be true. "Send me another picture," he demanded one day.

My heart started racing. How was I going to find another picture to send him? Since I was now supposedly the proud owner of a scanner, I had no excuse. So I went on another online scavenger hunt, this time to try to find a girl who resembled the fake me. I found one; she was light-skinned with curly hair and posed in the shower, half-naked. She looked like she could have been partially Asian. But the initial picture I sent him was black-and-white and the new picture of the girl in the shower was in black-and-white, so I figured that he wouldn't know the difference.

I was wrong. He confronted me on the phone. Partly amused, partly miffed.

"That's not your real picture, is it."

"Yes, it is."

"You look like two completely different people."

"People always tell me that when I curl my hair."

"I don't think either of these pictures are you."

"Yes, they are."

Not willing to argue with me about my fake identity, he pleasantly let me go. Ultimately, he stopped talking to me altogether. Lesson learned.

Eventually, the online conversations and fake adult sex no longer filled the void that my socially inactive middle school life had left wide open. My friends were being asked out. People were coupling up, and I was left with my lies and my fake personas. I needed someone to like me for me. Or at least who I pretended to be *in person*.

# FAT

According to everything I read in both women's and health magazines (those must be right, right?), I can look forward to obesity, diabetes, and horrible skin. That's my prognosis, should I continue to indulge my food addiction. I'd like to blame it on the "new money," i.e. money I'm now earning on my own as opposed to the money my parents have had to float me until recently—but even when I had *no* money, I still found a way to satiate my appetite for eating out. It's probably my mom's fault. After eighteen years of being limited to Fast Food Fridays (and sometimes Saturdays), I became obsessed with dining out. All the kids and teens on television had those hangout spots where they ate after-school junk food: The Max, The Peach Pit, The Honker Burger . . . the list goes on. Denied that as a kid, I *live* for social eating and, sometimes, solo social eating. (If people are around, people on my television screen included, that qualifies as "social eating" in my book.)

If conversation is something I dread, eating is something I look forward to. I wake up excited for breakfast, which is, hands down, my favorite meal of the day. Sometimes, at dinner, I fantasize about what I'm going to eat for breakfast the next morning. If it's the weekend, then I'll spend an hour or two reading glowing Yelp reviews as I research new brunch places. That's just my life.

Even during my financially challenged days, when my fridge was practically empty, I always had an abundance of either milk or eggs—both, on a pay week—which meant cereal, omelettes, and/or pancakes were always an option. And during those super-lazy and broke breakfast moments, when all I had were slices of bread and eggs—French toast! The homemade variety is a rare breakfast indulgence for me, as my mom treated French toast as a food of last resort, using the ends of the bread loaves she'd kept in the freezer for Thanksgiving stuffing to make hers. It was good, but I've definitely bitten into some freezer-burned French toast, much to my offense.

Moving to Los Angeles instigated another present-day fatty food obsession: Mexican food. Tortillas and beans and cheese—oh my! So much cheese. So many nachos. So many artery-clogging, delectable, filling foods that don't even exist in Mexico. Whoever concocted these "Mexican" treats, I love you.

Food is my destination, my journey, my reward, my friend—if only my metabolism matched that of the skinny, crackhead-bodied girls of my high school. How lucky they were! Many of them grew up to be the women who, even when pregnant, looked as if they had only protruding Tic Tacs in their stomachs, women who consumed food regardless of starch or sugar content without gaining an ounce. If my self-esteem weren't directly correlated to my BMI, my love affair with food would be positively nurturing. I could flaunt my love affair on Facebook and Instagram without shame, posting pictures of myself cuddled up with food. It would be a beautiful life.

But alas, in reality, I'm in a self-inflicted abusive relationship. I'm that thirsty girl who constantly checks for her "man," wondering about his whereabouts, desperate to see him again. Ironically, if I treated my food like I did my real-life relationships, I'd eat only when hungry. With my true love, food, I embarrass myself to no end to get its attention. As a result, my weight has fluctuated my entire life. In my high school and college years, I was in the plus-or-minus-ten-pounds range. In the latter half of my twenties, I've been more along the lines of the plus-or-minus-thirty-pounds range. What the hell is that? Why do I deserve that? Because as we women age our hormones change? Is that it? Mother F-You Nature.

As I write this, sipping on a vanilla milkshake from The Melt, I'm currently stretching the seams of the plus-thirty end of the spectrum and it is truly disgusting. I've resolved many times to force myself to get a grip, exercise, and eat right. "Don't turn into Kirstie Alley" is my personal mantra. As of late, I can last for six days maximum before I wild the fuck out. There's always a social gathering, an event, a Red Lobster commercial to expose my thinly veiled self-promises for what they really are: pathetic lies.

I have a plethora of self-esteem-damaging stories that should have put me on the straight-and-narrow path toward weight loss. And for a brief moment, they probably did. Like the time in seventh grade when my grandfather was set to pick me up after school because my mom was going to be stuck at the school where she taught French until late that evening. Despite knowing he was fastidiously punctual, I assumed that things would be different this time. I was in a new private school in Brentwood, California. The moving parking lot known as the 405 freeway was the most practical route to get to my school. Sure, you could take the streets if stop-and-go traffic made you feel more efficient, but the 405 was typically unavoidable.

Getting to Barrington by three in the afternoon would be difficult, I reasoned.

It was by this logic that when Allison, my school best friend and carpool buddy at the time (in hindsight, a frenemy), suggested we go get a slice at the popular pizza place up the hill, I agreed. I didn't even protest a bit: "No, I'm pretty sure my grandfather will be here and I'd hate to keep him waiting." Nope. As much as I'd love to blame peer pressure as an excuse, I simply can't. No suggestion of a food outing has ever elicited *any* protest from me. Ever.

So off we went, trekking up the hill, walking past the line of luxury cars filled with parents waiting to swoop up their kids. To my credit, I probably made sure to check the line of cars for my grandfather's 1987 golden Mercedes and newsboy hat, as Allison and I traded gossip about the day's events. Not seeing his car in line only validated my decision to round out the afternoon with a food excursion. By the time we reached the restaurant, ten minutes later, the line for ordering pizza snaked outside. That's when I started to get nervous. We'd be there for at least another thirty minutes just getting through the line. But the smell of pizza dough, garlic, and marinara sauce was enough to soothe my worries. Even if my grandfather was down there, he could wait. Where did he have to go anyway?

Forty-five additional minutes passed before we each got our order of a slice of pizza, a drink, and fries to go. By now, the sun had unexpectedly started to set. I'm always too lazy to figure out whether it's daylight saving or not. (All I know is I'm not a fan of the time change that has the sun right in your face when you wake up and takes it away at five o'clock in the afternoon. I don't give a damn if it gives me an extra hour of sleep; it is not worth the productivity of which it robs me.) As we made our way down the darkening hill,

I got a dreadful feeling in the pit of my stomach. The line of cars was long gone, and I could only see a few cars parked in the parking lot in the distance, one of which was the golden Mercedes that had once been my father's, the first car he had bought with his new eighties ob-gyn salary. If only I could walk up to the car and find him inside. He'd probably take some of my fries as punishment for being late and that would be that. But no, my dad had long since "upgraded" to a gray Saturn.

This would be my best frenemy's first time meeting my grandfather, and it began to dawn on me that they'd make a horrible first impression on each other.

Perhaps it was the way that I greeted my grandfather, with a smile and a peppy, "Hey Papa!" that sent him over the edge. Or maybe it was that I hadn't been considerate enough to get him anything to eat or drink. (Although he wouldn't be able to taste it anyway, as he had lost his sense of taste and smell during some odd sickness that he caught decades ago.) Or maybe it really was just the fact that he had probably spent over two hours in traffic, coming all the way from Inglewood, only to wait an additional hour for his greedy, greasy-faced, non-resisting-pizza-ass granddaughter. Yeah, that was probably it.

I opened the door and he didn't even bother to greet Allison, which was highly unusual for him since my grandfather was known for four things: his New Orleans drawl, his love of bow ties, his docile friendly charm, and his overreacting temper.

"Ah, where were you? Do you know how long I been waitin'?" he asked, skipping the charm and going straight for the temper.

"I'm sorry. I just went to get some pizza. I didn't know you were here."

"You went to get some pizza?!"

His pent-up irritation made his voice thunder with disdain. My grandfather was all for buying us fast food when we deserved it. "How 'bout some MackDonald's!" he'd offer my siblings and me whenever we'd come to visit. But if we *asked* for McDonald's or any other type of fast food, he'd shake his head violently and take to the kitchen, announcing, "We gon' make our *own* MackDonald's," as he added green peppers and onions to his homemade hamburger patty. *Yuck.*

Allison sat in the backseat, sipping her drink and watching in amusement as she munched on her fries like they were a bag of popcorn. My grandfather took a look at my plate of food, and then he said the unthinkable, confirming all the suspicions I had about myself yet was too afraid to admit.

"That's how come you gettin' to be so FAT," he declared, starting the car with disgust. In fact, the way he pronounced "FAT" sounded like he was clearing a clot of Russian phlegm out of his throat, readying to spit it on my slightly protruding seventh-grade gut. I was hot with embarrassment and shame. I couldn't even look at Allison in the backseat, already certain that she would go home to repeat this story to her older sister as they laughed at my expense. Of all the people to say that in front of, she was the worst one. But more than that, the confirmation from my grandfather that I was fat was a punch in the gut. Yet another reason why I didn't fit in; or why the boys in my school looked past me; or why I'd never be considered as pretty as my friends.

As we rode in silence on the car ride home and my eyes filled with tears, I looked out of my window into the night sky and made a silent plea for God to make me skinny. Then I took a bite of my cold slice of pizza and tried to chew quietly.

Moments like that (and more that followed) should compel me

to turn my life around, to starve myself, and to get myself in better physical shape. And for a time, I do. But then, I hit a wall. Sometimes it's a wall that I'll build for myself, and sometimes it's one that life builds for me. I've been my ideal weight only twice: one time was by accident and the other was the result of not eating food for ten days.

The first time I lost a noticeable (to everyone else but me) amount of weight was in high school, when I went to visit my relatives in Senegal after not having seen them for five years. (In case you missed the explanation of my name, my father is Senegalese.) I was fifteen and my parents sent my little brother, my little sister, and me off to Africa by ourselves, the first time we had ever traveled such a long distance without them. The morning after we arrived, my dad's side of the family gathered around the center outdoor terrace of our family home and made a huge deal about seeing us. My aunts, in particular, rejoiced about how fat my sister and I were.

"*Vous êtes pata!*" one aunt exclaimed. (Translation: "You guys are fat.")

"*Vous mangez bien la-bas,*" another aunt commented, laughing. (Translation: "You girls are eating well over there.")

This was both jarring and embarrassing.

Still, I made no conscious effort to reverse my weight. It was only a combination of diarrhea, the three-meal "eat what you can" plan, a lack of snacks, rigorous exercise (otherwise known as walking in the heat), and going clubbing at night (the clubbing age limit was sixteen) that effected a change I had no willpower to make on my own. Oh, and the fact that I had become a pescatarian just the year before, much to the confusion of my cousins, worked miracles.

"You don't eat meat . . . on purpose?" my older cousin asked.

"Yeah. Something I heard on the radio about how meat is processed and manufactured."

"But, that's the U.S. We don't do that here. You can eat meat made in Senegal. It's natural. It's halal," he tried to persuade me.

"No, thanks. I'm good."

"I wish we could afford to *not* eat something by choice," he mused.

When I came back to the States at the end of summer, I had a "cute shape" (my mother's words), having finally gotten rid of the baby fat that refused to grow the fuck up and move out of my body. My friends noticed the change. My new nickname was "skinny bitch." It was the best compliment I ever could have received and allowed me a new confidence. Yet just as I started to grow accustomed to my skinny curves, college and the Sophomore Twenty happened.

The second time in life that I lost a significant amount of weight, I was aided by being broke in New York. I had already lost a significant amount just by trying to survive with two part-time jobs in the city, but I still wasn't satisfied with my appearance. My younger siblings can attest to the fact that I've wanted a six-pack since I was in the sixth grade. I'm sure I could attribute this body image must-have to countless music videos featuring the perfect midriffs of TLC, Aaliyah, Destiny's Child, and Mya. Also, the fact that midriffs were in style in middle school, in my opinion thanks to *Clueless*.

Needless to say, I didn't accomplish that goal then. One spring, two years after college, however, everything changed. Five of my close friends and I decided to take a trip to the Dominican Republic together. A girls' trip. Half of us were single and half of us were not, but we were all determined to act as one cohesive, partying, semi-slutty unit. One of my friends was already notorious for her sixty-five albums on Facebook, full of memorable, oft-embarrassing pictures of me and my other friends. She could make or break your photo history. This thought alone made me resolve to look my best for this trip, better than I had ever looked before. I *had* to get in shape. So, I took on the Master Cleanse, a.k.a. the maple syrup, cayenne pepper, and lemonade diet, a.k.a. "the Beyoncé Diet," and gained an entirely new perspective on dieting.

I decided to take "before and after" pictures. Considering my previous life felt like a giant "before" picture, I could have selected *any* picture I wanted, but I wanted to do this right. I decided to take full-on, gutty-flabtastic front and profile pictures, to show the world what I was. I would keep those pictures on file as inspiration, and they wouldn't be seen by the public until *after* I'd demonstrated some progress.

Next, I decided to enlist my mother. How I convinced her is still a mystery to me. Maybe it was the guilt she felt for passing her notorious abdominal genes down to me.

"Haha," she'd say, poking my stomach, setting off an involuntary wave of mini-jiggles, "you got that from me."

Maybe she, too, shared my desire to wear midriff T-shirts *without* high-waisted jeans. Either way, she decided to join me.

"I'll do it with you. But only for four days."

And that was enough for me. Despite my hatred of group projects, I'm a collaborator. A team player. When it comes to difficult things that I *want* to accomplish, I'm all about working with people. Even writing. While there's a satisfaction that comes with completing something all by yourself, sometimes things are just more efficient and promising when you know that people are in the trenches, suffering with you.

So we embarked on our journey together and it was literally shitty. I ass-peed for the first time in my adult life. I got up to urinate frequently; my record was four times during an hour-and-a-half-long meeting. So as to distract myself from eating, I watched movies and online food videos. Watching other people eat on television was soothing. I used my blog to document my journey and attracted a slew of followers interested in my weight-loss journey. The rapid results surprised me. I posted a Before and After picture of my five-day progress, and there was a noticeable difference. I continued for five more days, for a total of ten days WITHOUT FOOD! I took my final After picture and I had a fucking six-pack. I had never seen my abs before that. I posted my proud pictures on Facebook, and my feed and blog exploded. People who had made fun of me for doing the diet before suddenly expressed a desire to try it. If approval can be judged by Facebook comments, let's say I passed expectation. Best of all, I was ready to proudly rock a bikini in the Dominican Republic.

Completing the Master Cleanse opened up a whole new door of masochism for me. I was now privy to my starvation limits and would undoubtedly subject myself to something of equal or greater suffering in the future, just to reach my body goals. Because once the compliments come in, you're totally seduced into equating self-worth with skinniness. *Wow, you look great! Oh my God, so skinny! Geez, what's your workout plan?* The compliments were the most *addictive* drug of all. I live for the validation that accompanies weight loss.

Moving to Los Angeles only intensified my need to be thin. Though fellow dieters seem to be everywhere and restaurants provide more "fit friendly" options, it took a more conscious effort on my part to stay in shape, as walking in L.A. is not an option. On top of which, as I started working consistently, I had more money, which meant more access to food. Rather than lose weight, I found my weight increasing. My comfort with food simply outweighed my determination to be a smaller size.

Then, at the end of 2013, after fourteen years of being a pescatarian, I had an epiphany while I was in the midst of the Earthbar Juice Cleanse. I had survived the cleanse for five whole days the year before, but this time, I kept it real with myself and decided that three days was enough. I had just come back from a weeklong East Coast trip, where I had eaten room service and pizza every single night and drank at least four out of the seven days I was traveling. I was already forty pounds heavier than I wanted to be and newly entering an industry where every extra pound matters. My body was begging me for a restart. So when I got back to L.A., I made a vow to change my ways. But something happened during the cleanse: I started watching marathons of *Chopped* and *Master Chef* and began to question why I stopped eating meat in the first place. I honestly couldn't recall. Then it all came back to me. I was in the ninth grade and my father had picked me up from school; NPR was playing on the radio, as always. About the same time we were assigned to read Upton Sinclair's *The Jungle*, I remember listening to a story about how meat was processed and what hot dogs were made of. Then and there, I decided to give up meat. Even my dad, whose regular palate matches that of a protein-craving pregnant woman's, declared that he would stop eating meat, too. The following day my last meat meal (on purpose, anyway) was chicken enchiladas. My dad's resolve was less firm. He continued to eat the hell out of all meat (except pork).

Now, nearly fifteen years later, after years of dealing with the confusion of my extended family and peers—"Not even chicken? Chicken doesn't count!"—I decided that I wanted bacon.

On the final day of my cleanse, I cleared my entire schedule to take a trip to Trader Joe's, Costco, and the Farmer's Market. I had to stop myself from picking up every single type of meat imaginable, but still came home with ground turkey, a Wagyu steak, chicken drumsticks, chicken breasts, and the most important of all: bacon.

Or so I thought. My entire life, my mother had restricted us from pork. As a girl, I thought it was out of respect for my father's religion. But when I grew older, I found out it was because my mother just didn't think pork was "clean." This logic didn't really matter to me, as I had resolved to stop eating all meat except fish anyway. But when standing in the aisle of Trader Joe's, deciding which type of nitrate-free, hormone-free, organically clean pack of bacon to choose, I opted for the *turkey* bacon—the kind with which we'd grown up.

That evening I returned to my apartment with bags of groceries, filled to the brim with meat, meat seasonings, and vegetables that taste good with meat. I couldn't even finish the final two vegetable juice cleanses I had paid for; my appetite had already transitioned. I could barely sleep that night, as I dreamt of my first breakfast meal, with its new addition: bacon.

I woke up at six in the morning and went straight to cooking. Scrambled eggs, sweet potato hash, and . . . dry turkey bacon. It didn't look like it did in all the food shows I had been watching, but now wasn't the time to nitpick. When I took that first bite and closed my eyes in ecstasy, it was as if I had never left the meat-eating world. It was the best bite of food I had ever eaten in my life. But looking back, I think my pleasure could be equated with one of my longtime abstinent friends getting laid on her wedding night and exclaiming how amazing sex was, even if, in fact, it had been only mediocre. Deep down, I knew there was better in my future. My mother's aversion to pork didn't have to be my own. Immediately after breakfast, I went back to the Farmer's Market and bought the real deal, pork-belly bacon. After *that* first bite, I began a new love affair with pork—I couldn't understand why it had such a horrible reputation, and I didn't care to.

Then the unthinkable happened. During my first month as a re-formed carnivore, I lost eleven pounds—*without* even working out or dieting. I don't regret my years as a vegetarian, by any means. Yet to think that the majority of my teenage and adult body issues could have been eliminated had I not been so faithful to the *one* dietary restriction I was ever disciplined enough to maintain is infuriating.

But like a lover you keep despite the mind games he plays, I can never stay mad at food for too long. In fact, I gotta go. I'm craving him now.

# ABG Guide: Public Grazing

My fellow awkwards, once you step foot out of your own home, expect to be seen. It's inevitable. It's taken me two whole decades to acknowledge this horrifying fact, and so now I'll trade the sweatpants for comfortable mom jeans and pat my 'fro down into a socially acceptable shape before leaving my apartment. It has nothing to do with self-respect, but rather a fear of being talked about, or snapped in someone's popular @shittyppllooklike Instagram. My fear of walking in front of a group of teenage black kids[1] has NOTHING on my fear of being watched while eating in public.

Living in New York slapped my fear of going out solo right out of me. I used to feel sorry for people eating alone at restaurants or going to the movies by themselves; I'd go so far as to pray that they'd

---

1 Having been a teenage black kid, I know firsthand how much we *loved* to laugh and talk shit about people, especially when sitting idly. I didn't always participate, but I recognized it as a form of entertainment and bonding. Knowing how ruthless some of my friends were and how haphazard I can be in my appearance, I tend to cross the street when I see groups.

find a companion to complete them. Then I moved to New York and witnessed millions of people content with doing things by themselves: grocery shopping, subway hopping, park benching, movie watching, restaurant dining. So many things to do alone without fear of any judgment. It was just the norm. I remember the first time I went to see "*Ne le dis à personne*" by myself at Landmark Sunshine Cinema. What an experience! I bought all the snacks I wanted: a medium popcorn, a vegan double-chocolate-chip-brownie cookie, Reese's Pieces, and a Diet Coke. Then I sat at the end of the aisle of a partially filled theater and propped my feet up on the seat in front me—HEAVEN! No one to ask me questions during the movie, no one threatening to predict what was going to happen next, no one to dip their spit-tipped fingers in my popcorn—just me and the movie. After that, a whole new life of self-imposed isolation opened up to me.

Instead of ordering food to go at my favorite Indian restaurant and carrying it home to eat in my tiny closet-sized room, whose walls would absorb the curried cauliflower smell for three days minimum, I would instead eat *inside* the overtly festive restaurant.

"How many, ma'am?"

"Just one!"

Though it took me a while to fully adjust, I was soon enough content with my phone or the book I had brought to read.

I would take this newfound joy to Los Angeles with me. If anyone felt such pity for me as I used to pity my fellow solo diners, I was oblivious. In fact, in some ways, New York made me embrace being alone. Don't misunderstand me; I don't want to die alone, but spending quality time with myself 60 to 70 percent of the day is my idea of mecca.

However, just as singing in the car with your windows rolled up tricks you into feeling as though you're truly socially isolated, it is very important to remember that even while eating solo, you are being watched. That offbeat dance you do in your car? Someone has laughed at you. That time you picked your nose in the park? It made someone gag. The way you shoveled food onto your fork with your index finger and then chewed it with your mouth open as chunks of spitfood fell back onto your plate prompted someone to regard you as a savage.

I don't consume food prettily while alone. It's all I can do to eat prettily in the company of suitors, when somehow I manage to keep it together just enough to keep them interested. When alone, I both surprise and disappoint myself with how fast I swallow food whole, sometimes to my detriment. Food frequently gets stuck in my throat and chest, often while I'm with company, at which point I lose the ability to talk, my eyes water, and I must go to the bathroom, stick my long, perfectly bulimic finger down my throat, and then cough it out. Then when my food-loving instincts kick in and send the proper "calm down, hungry, greedy bitch" signal to my stomach, I resume. If I'm lucky, this happens only once during the meal, and only when I eat dry foods like rice and poorly-cooked salmon.

If you share my fears and lack the social grace to eat, well, gracefully, practice being L.A.D.Y.-like. L.A.D.Y. stands for: Loner Artfully Digesting Yummies. This means, sit in the corner of a restaurant, facing a window, with your back to the rest of the patrons (you're doing them a service), and feel free to chow down. Be aware of the waiter coming to check up on you. Waiters see customers eat ugly all the time, but those people have *nothing* on you. That's what the window is for. Take time out of your busy, disgusting chomping to check your reflection every once in a while and to make sure the waiter doesn't sneak up on you while you have all the sanguine-colored condiments around your mouth and cheeks, like you've just ravaged a zebra carcass.

If this is too much for you to bear, and you can't eat food without making a mess and drawing attention to yourself, then your best bet is to make use of the "To Go" option. You're not ready to take advantage of the meditative quality of eating out alone just yet.

# Leading Lady

Several months ago, I was blocked on Twitter by a disabled, white stripper.

It was the night of the Grammys. I had just left a viewing party/ get-together and was a wee bit tipsy. Having witnessed the many talented performers and sexy dancers throughout the night, I was feeling lackluster and was in a self-deprecating mood. So with this fresh on my mind I tweeted, "*Sometimes I really wish I was[2] a stripper. But a respectable one. I would always start off wearing pantsuits and dance to [Queen Latifah's] 'U.N.I.T.Y.'*"

This tweet was earnest and, in my mind, harmless. Moments later, I scrolled my mentions, chuckling at the other rhythmless girls who felt my sentiments, before one tweet caught my eye. It

---

2 I only recently learned how to distinguish between "If I was" and "If I were" for the purpose of this book. Twitter does not merit such effort. Don't judge!

read: *"Wow. How BRAVE. Not like all us gross disrespectable sex workers."*

The hostility slapped me in the face, so I decided to check out the sender's time line, to understand how my tweet might have offended her. I read several of her tweets about how much she hates people, and how tired she is of everyone oppressing sex workers in our culture. I read multiple posts about how she was suffering from insomnia as well. As I continued to read through her hatred of all things human, I just knew that surely she couldn't be placing me in this category of hate. She must have been sleep-deprived and misunderstood my tweet. I responded:

*"We should talk about this in the morning when you get some sleep, Grumpy McGrumperson."*

And then she promptly responded:

*"We should talk about this when you get some empathy, you whore-phobic asshole."*

And that's when all hell and confusion broke loose, because I could have sworn that what I'd expressed fit the definition of social media empathy. I had looked at her time line, seen that she was sleep-deprived, and responded to her. But apparently it was insensitive empathy—if that even exists.

And then she blocked me and publicly added me to her ever-growing list of people that she hates. She compared the oppression of being a disabled sex worker to the oppression of being a person of color. *What is the difference between my oppression and your oppression?* she asked. At first I was amused. *What an extremely unpleasant and delusional stripper*, I thought. *Does she make the men and women she entertains feel guilty for enjoying themselves, too? Geez.* I went to bed that night thinking, *I doubt I could have learned any twerk tips from her anyway.* And then the more I thought about it over the next couple of days, the more her offense and her general anger got under my skin. Why was she so mad? What was it about what I said that triggered her? And what *did* we have in common, if anything?

As I perused her time line from another, unblocked account (*haha, loophole!*), I noticed how upset she was about the representation of "sex workers," as she called them, in the media. In all, it seemed she just wanted an accurate, fair representation of her field of work, as opposed to continuing to be the butt of jokes in television and film. At the very core of her anger was a desire to see a respectable reflection of herself.

I immediately thought of my absolute favorite Junot Díaz quote. He said:

> *You guys know about vampires? . . . You know, vampires have no reflections in a mirror? There's this idea that monsters don't have reflections in a mirror. And what I've always thought isn't that monsters don't have reflections in a mirror. It's that if you want to make a human being into a monster, deny them, at the cultural level, any reflection of themselves. And growing up, I felt like a monster in some ways. I didn't see myself reflected at all. I was like, "Yo is something wrong with me? That the whole society seems to think that people like me don't exist?" And part of what inspired me, was this deep desire that before I died, I would make a couple of mirrors. That I would make some mirrors so that kids like me might see themselves reflected back and might not feel so monstrous for it.*

Isn't that the realest shit ever?

———————

The first screenplay I ever wrote was called *Judged Cover*, about a chubby, unattractive, black high school girl who gets her first breakout role in a movie. She deals with an unsupportive mother, starts hanging with the wrong Hollywood crowd, turns to drugs, and eventually commits suicide. It was shitty and sad, but I was so proud of it. I remember giving it to Monique, one of my best friends, to read, and the next school day she came back and asked, "Are you going to play the lead?" I planned on it. The script wasn't autobiographical by any means, but I could relate to feeling too unattractive to play a leading lady. Also, the fact that she recognized that I could play the pathetic character I had written only confirmed my insecurity.

Ten years later I saw *Precious*, and I remember thinking it was *Judged Cover* on steroids. WHO THE FUCK'S LIFE WAS *THAT*?! I sat in the theater with my two best friends, Jerome and Devin, fuming as the final scene played. Not because I disliked the film, not because I couldn't relate to the story, but because Hollywood was so fucking excited about this movie.

I remember turning to my friends after the film and saying, "From now on, I'm going to end all of my complaints with, '. . . but at least I'm not Precious.' " We spent the rest of the day grateful that we were not Precious. But then I thought, is *that* was it takes to create a sympathetic black female lead character? I could imagine the boardroom meeting.

*She has to be obese!*

*She has to be super poor.*

*She has to be illiterate!*

*She has to have an abusive mother who molests her.*

*She has to be a rape victim of her FATHER!*

*She has to be teenage and pregnant.*

*She has to be HIV positive.*

*She has to have a baby with Down syndrome!*

*Now* we care about this lead character. *Oh my God, she's so tragic. Oh my God, the ghetto. Oh heavens, what a cautionary tale! Oh to be black and poor in the ghetto. No wonder they're so mad and defensive all the time.*

*Precious* was the anti–Tyler Perry, Tyler Perry–co-produced black film of the year and one of the many straws that broke the camel's back (my camel is a masochist). While I was grateful for our introduction to the amazing Gabourey Sidibe (Senegal, stand up!), I needed to see more from my movies than the extremely tragic black woman, or the magic helpless Negro, or the many black men in dresses.

You could say I have an entertainment complex. It stems from growing up during the golden age of nineties television. I look back and realize what a huge and amazing influence it was to have an array of diverse options to watch almost every night of the week. *The Cosby Show* was a variation of my own family—my doctor dad, my teacher mom, and my four siblings. *A Different World* made me want to go to college, talk about smart-black-people stuff, and find my own Dwayne Wayne. (As an aside, I looked for Dwayne's double shades forever, and when I finally found them in the late nineties, nobody was checking for me. Their loss.) The nineties produced *The Fresh Prince of Bel-Air*, *All That*, *Living Single*, *Kenan & Kel*, *New York Undercover*, *Martin*, *All-American Girl*, *Moesha*, and *Family Matters* (Does anybody know what the hell happened to Judy? She went upstairs and literally got grounded for life.). Nineties television produced a plethora of images of people of color, and don't even get me started on all the different film options we had. It was encouraging. Back in the nineties, we were relatable. Audiences cared about what we had to say and studios recognized our value, at least as far as ad revenue was concerned.

Then as the decade made way for the new millennium, cable exploded with its own original content and film studios began to obsess over international box office sales. Somewhere along the line, we became unrelatable and invisible to the Hollywood system. Our images and diverse portrayals just weren't worth the dollars and effort anymore. The images I had grown up with and grown so accustomed to seeing slowly disappeared, and it seemed to happen all at once. When I was in Potomac as the sole black girl, these shows were my access to black culture in some ways. When I moved to Los Angeles and the kids said I talked white but had nappy hair, I found a sort of solace in knowing that Freddie from *A Different World* and Synclaire from *Living Single* were napped out, too. I could be worse things.

Right around the time I moved to Los Angeles, my passion for writing increased. I was in the hub of film and television and felt a need to take advantage of this, as quickly as possible. Also around that time, the new Cosby show came out on CBS. Since I related to the first show so much, I decided to write a spec script and send it to CBS. The episode, called "The Tongue Ring," centered around Cosby's character coming to terms with his daughter's suggestive new piercing. (It was 1996 and I was eleven, so tongue rings were still very controversial.) I showed the script to my grandmother, who happens to be very computer savvy, and she encouraged me to submit it, so I did. It took nothing but a general internet search to find the address and BOOM, my talent was out there. Not wanting to put all my eggs in one basket, I wrote another television pilot, called *Ronnie*, a high school dramedy about gang violence, kind of like the short-lived television show *South Central*. I looked up NBC's address, wrote a cover letter about how much I enjoyed their programming (*Saved by the Bell*, *California Dreams*, and *City Guys*), and sent it off. Though I got no response, I continued middle school content that I'd tried and optimistic that I'd have plenty of other shots in the future.

In high school, I developed a new love: acting. I went to a pre-dominantly black and Latino school in Compton and, outside of television, this was my first true immersion in black culture. I had an inspiring drama teacher, a Jewish man who found the most amazing, hidden plays of color. There was *On Striver's Row*, a play about an upper-middle-class black family in Harlem. *Maricela de la Luz Lights the World*, a fanciful and mystical Latino drama by José Rivera. And so much more. Every year for four years I was introduced to new diverse works, all while working with a multicultural cast. I only wish Hollywood could take a lesson from Compton.

The last great black film made in the nineties (released in April 2000) was *Love & Basketball*, a beautiful love story shot in my neighborhood. Even as I watched that movie at my friend's sleepover, I was completely aware that it was shaping my mind and changing my life. It was the very first time I had seen a woman who was just "normal black" on-screen. Though Sanaa Lathan was absolutely beautiful, she played an around-the-way girl, a tomboy like me. I felt as if I could be her.

So began my fixation. I watched the film again before I left my friend's house, then set out to buy it on DVD. The ultimate game-changer for me was when I discovered that it was written and directed by a black woman, Gina Prince-Bythewood. I had never cared to listen to a DVD commentary for any other film prior, but I listened as she discussed the behind-the-scenes trials of making her film. I listened as she discussed Spike Lee's involvement and was inspired and grateful that he had played a role in making this film happen. Most important, I set out to write my own movie, *Judged Cover*.

While I was writing the screenplay, I realized it was five years since I had written anything original. I found the letters I wrote to CBS and NBC and decided to write to Gina Prince-Bythewood. Maybe she would have interest in my screenplay? How amazing would it be if she directed it? I grew excited. I typed her a letter and to this day I don't remember how or where I got her address. I wrote her about how much I loved the film, how much it inspired me, how I watched it every day for inspiration (I really did), and then I told her about *Judged Cover* and asked her if she would consider directing it. I didn't send her the script, because I hadn't finished it, and knew that was inappropriate to do so without solicitation. I waited.

The summer came upon us and I prepared to go to Dakar, Senegal, for the first time in five years. I checked my email the week before we left and gasped, ecstatically. She had written back! I still have the email from 2001:

Jo-Issa,

Thank you so much for your letter. It means a lot that *Love and Basketball* is your favorite movie! Much props to you for having a completed screenplay at sixteen. I didn't start writing scripts until I was in college. You definitely seem focused and know where you're going. I am flattered that you thought of me to direct your script, unfortunately, I am pretty much tied up for the next couple years with my own scripts. After directing "Disappearing Acts," which I didn't write, I realized I feel much more fulfilled as an artist when I direct scripts I have written myself, like "Love and Basketball." This does not mean I will never direct another script I or my husband has written, however, for now that is what I am focused on. That, and my new son. :) But again, thank you so much for thinking of me and good luck in all your endeavors.

Sincerely,

Gina Prince-Bythewood

It was the perfect encouragement I needed to take my script with me on my trip abroad. I impressed my Senegalese cousins with my index note cards and my printed pages, which I wrote during our many moments of humid boredom. I was going to be the screenwriter and star of my very own movie!

Except I never finished the script. I kept writing and rewriting to the point of frustration, and let the project fall by the wayside until eventually I just pushed it to the back of my mind.

By the time I got to college, reality television had taken over. Shows like *Flavor of Love* and *I Love New York* paved the way for the trashy, raunchy depictions of women of color we see in shows today, like *Basketball Wives* and *Love & Hip Hop*. By the time college hit, I had already gotten used to seeing us only in rare glimpses. My sensibilities started to gear more toward shows like *Curb Your Enthusiasm*, *The Office*, *Seinfeld*, and *30 Rock*—all of which were generally devoid of leading characters of color. With the expansion of Netflix, my movie tastes began to broaden and I noticed that the more I explored genres outside of comedy and drama, the less and less I saw people of color. So I started to search for more stories of color, which was where I rediscovered Spike Lee's *School Daze*. I had heard about the film through my mother and my aunt, who frequently referenced the "Good and Bad Hair" scene. Watching the film alone, in my college dorm room my freshman year, was a pivotal and wholly new experience for me, coming as it did when I was losing interest in the limited kinds of productions my school's drama department was mounting.

Having been an active member of my high school's drama department, I figured my transition to college productions would be just as seamless. It wasn't. In fact, I didn't really fit into Stanford's drama department. The plays they put on were super white and so were their leads. If it weren't for Debi, an ambitious junior I met who decided to put up a self-penned Hip-Hopera, I don't know that I would have pursued theater at Stanford. She cast me as one of her leads, raised money through Stanford's many opportunities for student funding, and marketed it via our various email lists (and posted flyers the old-fashioned way); in other words, she produced it herself. I was so impressed and inspired; part of me felt like if she could do it, why couldn't I?

With Spike Lee's *School Daze*, I tried my hand at directing and producing a stage version. Looking back, I had *no* idea what I was doing, but directing and producing gave me a sense of control that I didn't have as an actress. I was literally waiting to act, waiting for the roles, waiting for the call. Furthermore, I was coming to the conclusion that I could never and would never be a leading lady. Not in this industry. So I took my place comfortably and happily behind the scenes, content to create the content that was otherwise absent during my college experience. Not to mention being behind the scenes and directing *other* actors made me realize how much I was lacking as an actress myself. I had a new appreciation for my high school director. Working with and organizing a group of thirty people was hard enough when people took our project seriously; I can't imagine having to direct a group of half-hearted teenagers. In any case, Stanford gave me the opportunity to put my own spin on theater, and to learn by doing. My plays were met with ongoing enthusiasm and encouragement, with the three shows we'd put on for one weekend consistently packed every year.

By the time I was a senior, I was known for my plays. It felt good to have a sense of identity and to have established myself as a director and producer. But it wasn't all smooth sailing. During my senior year, while others were taking it easy, I found that I had to take twenty-two units during my last two quarters to graduate on time. As much as I loved and appreciated Stanford for exposing me to the most amazing community I had ever experienced, it was time to get out of there and move on. I refused to stay an additional year to finish the last two units I needed to graduate (an online class at Santa Monica College would eventually earn me my diploma).

It was during this extremely stressful course load that I came up with the idea to do a web series about what it's like to be black at Stanford University. Stanford really opened my eyes to how diverse we are as a people,[3] and it was so refreshing to witness. I rounded my friends together, borrowed a camera from the library, and wrote a script. The next week, I edited it and posted it to Facebook and watched as it spread not only throughout my school, but at other top schools like Duke, Harvard, and Georgetown. People exclaimed that it reflected their college experience and marveled at how relatable it was. I couldn't believe the series had spread and that people who didn't attend my school were watching and enjoying. Having direct access to an audience that appreciated my work was an epiphany for me.

In the meantime, I felt surrounded by the mainstream media's negative images of black women. This was all prior to the promising Shonda Rhimes takeover of Thursday nights, so as the negative portrayal of women in reality television broadened its boundaries, I grew angry, resentful, and impatient. How hard is it to portray a three-dimensional woman of color on television or in film? I'm surrounded by them. They're my friends. I talk to them every day. How come Hollywood won't acknowledge us? Are we a joke to them?

---

3 Refer to ABG Guide: Connecting with Other Blacks for an appendix of the various blacks.

Now, having been in the industry for a couple of years, I'm not entirely sure it's blatant racism, as I had once assumed. It's more complicated than that. As Ralph Ellison once posited, we're invisible to them. We're simply not on their radar. As long as the people who are in charge aren't us, things will never change.

*Girls*, *New Girl*, *2 Broke Girls*. What do they all have in common? The universal gender classification, "girl," is white. In all three of these successful series, a default girl (or two) is implied and she is white. That is the norm and that is what is acceptable. Anything else is niche.

If it weren't for YouTube, I would be extremely pessimistic, but I'm not anymore. YouTube has revolutionized content creation. If it weren't for YouTube, I would still be at studios trying to convince executives that Awkward Black Girls really do exist. If it weren't for YouTube, I would have been indefinitely discouraged by the network executive who suggested that actress/video girl/Lil Wayne's baby's mother, Lauren London, would be a great fit for the title character of a cable version of Awkward Black Girl. If it weren't for social media, I don't know that black women would even be a fully formed blip on the radar. If it weren't for internet forums and fan pages, communities of dark women wouldn't be empowered by their natural hair in a media society that tells them their hair should be straightened and their skin should be lighter.

Online content and new media are changing our communities and changing the demand for and accessibility of that content. The discussion of representation is one that has been repeated over and *over* again, and the solution has always been that it's up to us to support, promote, and create the images that we want to see. Ten years ago, making that suggestion would have required *way* more work than it does now, and my love of taking shortcuts probably wouldn't allow me to make any dents on that front. But with ever-evolving, new accessible technologies, there are so many opportunities to reclaim our images. There's no excuse not to, and I've never felt more purposeful in my quest to change the landscape of television.

At the time I came up with the concept for ABG, I was just a clumsy, frustrated, socially inept, recently graduated adult, looking for confirmation that I wasn't alone. No, I didn't think I was a monster or vampire, Junot; it wasn't that deep. But at some level, as each new model for social media strives to connect us in new, paradoxically estranged ways, there exists a consistent core, the human desire to feel included. Whether you're an awkward black girl or an irritated disabled stripper, everyone should have the opportunity to feel represented in some way.

# ABG Guide:
# Connecting with Other Blacks

The gamut of "blackness" is so wide. So very, very wide. Luckily for you, I have encountered almost *every* type of black, and as the self-appointed representative of the "Awkward" Black, I am taking it upon myself to not only introduce other Awkward Blacks to each type of black, but also to give them guidance on appropriately dealing with each type. Take note: some blacks are a hybrid of two or even *three* blacks, though statistically that group is very small. In such cases, more than one interaction in more than one environment is required to determine the appropriate approach. Many blacks have been *all* of these blacks at one point in time. So as not to place the importance or value of one black over the other (that's what real life is for!), I have (more or less) organized them alphabetically. If you're not an Awkward Black, you may still find the information useful when attempting to engage other blacks.

––––––––

## The 10% Black:

W. E. B. Du Bois only added fuel to the fire for these blacks. The self-proclaimed talented tenth, these blacks feel as though the intellectual integrity of all blacks rests on their shoulders. Many are outwardly bitter that they have to carry this responsibility, but secretly appreciative that they have been called out as the Chosen Few. Usually the validation of one's tenthness comes from white acceptance. The 10 percent are both grateful for and resentful of this. The 10 percenters feel it is their duty to redeem blackness in the eyes of all.

**THE APPROACH:** Feign ignorance. You don't know as much as they do. If they deem you worthy, they will try to keep you at length and flex their knowledge, speaking *at* you. I've been caught for hours, listening to these blacks lecture. The key is to appear disengaged and dumb. It will save you time.

**KEY PHRASES:** "I don't know"; "Really?"; "Where's the chicken?"; "Cast down your bucket."

## The Ambitious Black:

Race isn't a barrier for this black; it's either an asset or not a concern at all. This black is a chameleon, able to turn it on and turn it off in any environment in the name of advancement. This black acknowledges his or her blackness to other blacks, but will quickly renounce race in front of "others." The Awkward Black and the Ambitious Black are very compatible.

**THE APPROACH:** The Awkward Black can find a potential friend and/or lover in this black. The Ambitious Black is the perfect partner to help the Awkward Black adjust in his/her own skin. For general interactions, be friendly and keep an eye open, because this black is studying and will take your job.

KEY PHRASES: "Let's hang"; "Teach me"; "Want to be my friend?"; "Love me."

## The Awkward Black:

*You Are Here.*

THE APPROACH: See entire book.

## The Basic Black:

Many confuse being "basic" with being "regular." That is false. "Regular" implies that there is a black norm, and I would argue that there is not. Barring strong innate familial traits and twins, blacks are not the same. The Basic Black, however, is the closest you can get to regular. The Basic Black is minimalist art in human form. People in this category are proud to be black, but don't flaunt it. They enjoy chicken and watermelon just as much as they enjoy steak and persimmons. Though goal-oriented, they are not complicated, and that is all there is to that.

THE APPROACH: Don't overcomplicate them. Talk to them as you would talk to your neighbor.

KEY PHRASES: "How are you?"; "How's the fam?"; "Have a nice day"; "Where's the BBQ?"

## The Hustling Black:

These blacks are a subcategory of the Ambitious Black, though they aren't quite there yet. Always "on the grind," this black has tried it all, has ridden every wave in an attempt to make ends meet. This black is on the move constantly, so don't ever try to ask him what he does, specifically. The answer will always vary. A Jack-of-all-trades but master-of-none, this black is still figuring everything out in his attempt to find a place in this world.

**THE APPROACH**: Encourage this black to find a focus, but show your support along the way.

**KEY PHRASES**: "Sure, we can do lunch"; "Yes, I'll listen to your new idea"; "Fine, I'll donate to your Kickstarter."

## The Insecure Black:

Constantly concerned with how race plays a factor in their everyday life, these blacks get really uncomfortable when race is brought up, fearing that all eyes will be on them. *Does everything have to be about race?* they ask. They don't offer opinions about Obama for fear of appearing biased. They listen to *all* genres of music, but generally try to stay away from hip-hop and R&B, as they don't want to be categorized. Their biggest fear is the return of slavery or a mutiny against blacks.

**THE APPROACH**: This black doesn't want to rock the boat, so broach general subjects, like academia and pop culture. But make sure the references aren't too loaded. So don't ask if Miley Cyrus is appropriating black culture when she twerks. Also avoid hip-hop in general, and Kim K.

**KEY PHRASES**: "What's the latest in *Popular Science* news?"; "Aren't babies cute?"; "The weather has been great/not so good."

## The Know-It-All About Blacks Black:

You might think I fall into this category, but I can assure you I don't. These blacks insist they know all there is to know about blacks, where they came from and where they're going. You may let it slip that you want to take swimming lessons. Mistake! The KIAAB Black will be quick to tell you that "black people don't swim." Do you have an idea that may progress the state of intra-racial relations? Don't bother. KIAAB Blacks tends to be super-pessimistic about our future and resist anything new. They are happy to list everything that black people *don't* do.

**THE APPROACH:** The Awkward Black is too outside-the-box for the Know-It-All About Blacks Black to comprehend. If you're black and say something a Know-It-All disagrees with, be prepared to be called white or whitewashed. For the general population, the KIAAB Black probably doesn't want to associate with you. He/She is content with sitting back and judging you. There's literally nothing you can do about it. Nothing.

**CONVERSATION TIPS:** Avoid talking and don't bother trying to change this black's mind about anything.

## The LGBT Black:

Just like blackness itself, the scope of the LGBT Black varies. Often torn between allegiances to two worlds, the LGBT Black finds him/herself at the bottom of the priority totem pole in both cases. Undervalued, unappreciated, and dismissed, many LGBT Blacks have a razor-edged chip on their shoulders. Others are perfectly content with who they are and are especially content with telling all of their business to anyone who will listen.

**THE APPROACH:** Don't bring up their sexuality if they don't. If they do, engage. Don't pry. Don't judge. Don't try to set them up with your friends. Don't assume gender. Don't show your privilege. Don't be misogynistic. Don't be homophobic. Don't be transphobic. Don't be cissexist. Just STFU, STFU, STFU.

**KEY PHRASE:** "I value you."

## The Militant Black:

Extremely proud to be black. For the Militant Black, everything is about race. This black experiences both pride and paranoia. This black has experienced racism at every turn and refuses to let you succumb to the same. Some militants are very hostile toward whites. Some are even bigoted where other ethnicities and nationalities are concerned. This black is often a Muslim convert and typically celebrates Kwanzaa and scoffs at you for celebrating white Jesus's Christmas.

**THE APPROACH:** In your attempts to appear tolerant, be wary of what comes out of your mouth to this black.

**CONVERSATION TIPS:** Hold back—everything you say can and will be used against you and misconstrued.

## The Nerdy Black:

Not to be confused with the Awkward Black, though some elements are interchangeable. The Nerdy Black is often socially hopeless. Where the Awkward Black constantly questions the social elements, often uncomfortably, the Nerdy Black is oblivious to any social cues whatsoever. Nerdy Blacks generally appreciate the crevices of pop culture. Science fiction, fantasy, fan fiction, reddit, conventions, video games—these things are all associated with nerd culture. Never underestimate the potential of the Nerdy Black.

**THE APPROACH:** Don't be judgmental of this black. For the Awkward Black, a beautiful friendship can be formed if you take the time to listen and learn. Awkward Blacks may find themselves the love interest of the Nerdy Black. You needn't be afraid. These blacks understand what it's like to be considered an outcast. Be gentle. For the general population, try not to confuse the Nerdy Black with hipsters. Nobody cares about hipsters and they don't even deserve a category.

**KEY PHRASES:** "I get you"; "No, I haven't heard of _____; please inform"; "I'm not making fun of you, I promise."

## The Not-Black Black:

They're quick to say, "Oh, I'm not black." My favorite type of Not-Black Blacks claims to be Native American. "That's why my hair is so good," they'll say. But ask them what tribe and they'll either fall short or claim "Cherokee." Oftentimes, the Not-Black Blacks are international. They tend to dissociate themselves from the shame associated with being "Regular" Black, unaware that there is no such thing. The stigma of being "black" is too much to bear, so they would rather not. These Not-Black Blacks are typically Caribbean, African, not American, and/or mixed Americans.

THE APPROACH: Don't make jokes. This black is serious. Play along or back away.

KEY PHRASES: "Your nose looks so European"; "Your hair is so silky and curly"; "I would never have thought you were black."

## The Position-of-Power Black:

This black is typically a hybrid. Unfortunately, however, the wee bit of power granted to this black eclipses all other personalities. Positions of Power can range from security guards/police officers to executives. Many times, the POP Black relishes the ability to turn other blacks away, dripping with condescension at every opportunity. The POP Black's asshole tendencies do not discriminate; power is power, and they will make you aware of this at every turn. However, POP blacks *do* tend to be harder on blacks so as to demonstrate that they are not discriminating.

THE APPROACH: Keep your words to a minimum and do NOT smile.

CONVERSATION TIPS: They don't enjoy conversations. Keep it moving.

## The Ratchet Black:

Previously known as "The Ghetto Black" or "The Hoodrat Black," these blacks are always pitted as black embarrassment. They are generally referred to as the Bottom-of-the-Barrel Blacks. Shaped by their environment, they are frequently feared and misunderstood.

THE APPROACH: Put on your Black-cent, if you have one. If your Black-cent isn't natural, don't force it; Ratchet Blacks will sniff you out. Make eye contact; don't act superior, because you're not. Don't be intimidated; just be yourself. If they don't sense an immediate connection, *they* will walk away from *you*, because you are weird.

KEY PHRASES: "Okay, girl"; "I know that's right"; "For real"; "I love Beyoncé."

## The Strong Black:

This black is tired from carrying the world on his or her shoulders. The Strong Black typically comes from a single-parent household and is used to getting things done on his or her own. Public emotions are rarely emitted from this particular black. Movies, in particular, love to exhibit and portray the Strong Black. One doesn't question what they've been through to make them so strong; we just accept their emotionless state as is.

THE APPROACH: These blacks are extremely reliable, but why would you want to add to the burden they already carry? Offer help and a listening ear when you can. They will be appreciative.

KEY PHRASES: "What's on your mind?"; "Can I help you with that?"; "Would you like some ice cream?"

## The Woe-Is-Me Black:

These blacks will never shut the hell up about their plight. They are victims, tortured by their blackness. Every ailment, struggle, and mistreatment is directly correlated with the color of their skin and their entire lives are tragedies. Victims are typically in the category of Tragic Mulatto/Quadroon/Octoroon/Quintroon/Hexadecaroon.

**THE APPROACH:** If you want to have a prosperous, joy-filled day, avoid these blacks at all costs. If you're cornered by one, briefly sympathize as you walk away. Sympathy is the key, not empathy, as you can never understand all that they have endured.

**KEY PHRASES:** "Aw, man"; "Yeah, that sucks"; "Oh nooo"; "I'm so sorry you're black."

————

As time moves forward and blackness expands, many of these blacks may become obsolete (some will undoubtedly be relieved). Until then, please carry this list with you everywhere, so as to promote the harmony of intra- and interracial race relations. The onus is on you.

# When You Can't Dance

Anyone who knows me personally, or even remotely, knows that I can't dance. It's sad. I just cannot. No matter how many Twerk Team videos I watch on YouTube, I can't isolate my booty in a way that rappers would find acceptable. And it's always been expected of me (see situations #1 and #2 in "The Struggle").

Being the only American girl in my Senegalese elementary school, I was asked:

"Jo-Issa, teach us what they do in the States!"

Being one of the few African-American girls in a gifted, nerdy elementary school in Potomac, Maryland, I overheard:

"Jo-Issa knows how to do the running man, right?"

I don't think it was until I met my first friend in Los Angeles that I realized I didn't dance the way some of the other black girls in my school did.

I'm not horrible. On a scale of Michael Jackson to Drunk White Girl, I come in at Drunk Black Girl. I can keep time really well.

I have great rhythm and can bounce to said rhythm accordingly. But seeing the way girls in my middle school moved and swayed their bodies like the women I sometimes noticed in adult music videos like "Rump Shaker" was a shock to me. Was I supposed to preternaturally know how to dance like this already? Was there a course I wasn't privy to? Had I known the social advantage to the dance classes my mother attempted to enroll me in, hoping to dilute my tomboy tendencies, I'd have obliged. But I refused. Even now, I can't go to a Zumba class filled with old Latina women without feeling self-conscious and inadequate.

It's not just that I couldn't put my hands on my knees, pop my booty, and do the Tootsie Roll, but this freak-dancing phenomenon was intimidating. I hadn't even seen a guy's privates before, and now I was required to put my butt on some random boy's junk and gyrate in an attractive way while he stood there? For the benefit of whom? Looking back at some of the dances we did in middle school and college, I realize they resembled animalistic mating calls. I can easily imagine Morgan Freeman narrating some of my high school dances. And with that same voice pointing out that my particular mating dance was unappealing to the entire male high school population.

Yes, past experiences had taught me to never again shine a light on my dance moves. Besides, nobody in my family is particularly gifted in dance. We all just "get by."

My sophomore year of high school, however, I felt a lot of pressure riding on me to be social, so I pretended that I knew how to dance. I was in an entirely different environment from my private school experience at Brentwood and had worked hard to be labeled as "the smart girl" at King/Drew High School of Medicine and Science, to which I had transferred. I could have left it at that. Yet part of me wasn't satisfied with being known as just that. I had met other "smart girls" and rapidly came to the conclusion that they didn't have much else to them. And I knew I did.

I wasn't ungrateful for my new smart status, but "smart" doesn't come with the same respect that "cool" does when you're in high school. If I could dance, though? OMFG. I would rule the school. Brains and moves? I'd be like my good friend Daisy. It was truly unfair how she had it *all*. Looks, brains, and moves. Why couldn't I be like that? I'd already given up in the looks department, but if I could dance, then at least eyes would be on me with a newfound respect.

So, one fateful I-don't-know-what-I-was-even-thinking day . . . I decided to lie. It happened when Lakira, one of the most popular (and sexually experienced) girls in school, who I was forming a relationship with, asked me in Algebra II class if I was going to her party. I blurted, "Yup." And she was pleasantly and happily surprised. Up until that point, I had managed to skip out on homecoming, the lunch dances, the formals, and anything else that related to dance. I knew from my years at Brentwood that if I could be outdanced by the Asians, I had no business showing my ass to my black peers. But something in me wanted to prove my worth to them. And so when Lakira pressured, "Can you even dance?" I boasted, "Uh . . . yes. You'll see. I get down."

Of course, it was precisely at that moment that the whole room quieted down, and most of the class heard my boastful admission. My other classmates chimed in.

"You can dance? I don't believe it."

"I can't even *imagine* you dancing."

As my neck and cheeks grew hot with anxiety and embarrassment, I continued the ruse. "Well, I guess you won't have to imagine when you come to the party."

They ate it up. And I took immense pride in my classmates' interest in this new hidden talent of mine. It was on, and I had flipped the switch to either my social embrace or my social execution; time would tell.

The clock was ticking and I had to learn to dance in eight days. Not *only* that, but I had to find an outfit that would be acceptable to present to my name-brand-idolizing peers. At King/Drew, we all wore black, white, and gold uniforms. This was torture for the stylish kids, who were bursting at the seams to show off their expansive wardrobes. There was so much teen angst associated with how restrictive our school uniforms were, yet while I feigned inconvenience with the best of them, secretly, I was grateful that I didn't have to go through what I went through in middle school. T.J.Maxx and Ross had name-brand knockoffs, but finding young people clothes that didn't look like they came from three seasons ago was a challenge. With the convenience of our uniforms, all my mom had to worry about were my shoes, and those were easy enough to keep name brand. Cute? No. Not with my size 11/12 feet, but name brand nonetheless. Nikes, Adidas, Chuck Taylors, and dress shoes of any kind were allowed, as long as they were black, white, or gold. (While FILA was name brand, *those* were for the Mexicans, I quickly learned from racist black high schoolers.)

For my formal dance training, I watched *106 & Park* daily (this was back when it was hosted by Free and AJ's velociraptor braids). I was already a fan of the show's Freestyle Friday segment, but my self-imposed eight-day course to learn how to dance required watching every music video with close attention to detail. I didn't have a television in my room, and as this was before YouTube was overpopulated with music videos and dance tutorials, I had limited options. I had to practice in the living room, which meant securing the space from anyone else's use, while masking from my younger brother and sister the fact that I was teaching myself to dance. They didn't need more fodder to use against me; they were already witty enough with their comebacks.

This was all during a time when Dancehall was growing mainstream on account of Sean Paul's "Gimme the Light" video. Those dances were *so* sick. Many of my classmates were just being introduced to this type of dance, so I imagined the playing field was pretty level. If I were to get a leg up edgewise, then I could have a shot. I imagined myself as one of the solo dancers in the video *killing* it at Lakira's party (specifically, the young, limber lady with the yellow midriff top and split bell-bottom pants). To this day, I've never been to a party where the room turns into a circle and select attendees get in the middle to perform freestyle dance moves. In my experience, nobody fucking cares enough to step aside and watch you dance. A fight? That's circle-worthy. Not "Save the Last Dance" moves. And yet all my dancing fantasies revolve around this essential party group formation.

The more I practiced in front of the television, the less I practiced in front of a mirror, which would have been the wise thing to do all along. Instead, in a self-imposed final exam, I tried out my moves in my mother's vast bathroom mirror, which didn't allow me to see my feet, but at least featured my whole upper body. I started out simply at first, keeping the rhythm and bouncing to the beat; then I pretended that I was the Dancehall Queen and after several poor gyrations, settled for being a Dancehall Lady-in-Waiting instead.

That Friday, when I came to school, all my friends were talking about their outfits for Lakira's party on Saturday. In all my dance fuss, I had forgotten about the second-most-important element of the party: my outfit.

My mother was generally encouraging of my social outings, so long as she knew the company I kept. Convincing her to give me more money on top of my weekly allowance to buy an outfit didn't prove to be as difficult as I thought it would, as long as I completed my assigned Saturday morning chores with polished haste. (My mother was always impressed with my cleaning and organizational skills. If I had decided to become a professional housekeeper, I don't know that she would have opposed. She recognizes my ability to bring order as a gift to others.) Getting a ride from my mother proved to be a harder task. Saturdays were her day to unwind after a trying school week, and anything that required her to do *anything* selfless was regarded as unpaid labor. Eventually, I convinced her to drop me off at the mall, where my tunnel vision was in full effect. I absolutely needed a jean jacket. My peers owned jean jackets of varying name brands, but my budget was limited to Charlotte Russe and the Juniors section at Macy's and Nordstrom's. Up Against The Wall, a trendy store that featured a live DJ and carried the biggest urban brands like Iceberg, Sean John, and Rocawear, was off limits for me. Nonetheless, I passed by the store to check out the guys and the clothes some of my peers were rocking. The blasting music only reminded me of my impending dance of doom. What song would I choose to humiliate myself to? "Back That Thang Up" was still a huge a hit; would it be that? Would I try to back it up to a Cash Money classic or would I try to keep it West Coast and Crip Walk to Kurupt? Naw, the party was taking place in South Central, and I still hadn't mastered the appropriate gang-color sections. I was far too lazy to color coordinate for the benefit of the surrounding color-obsessed gang members. But I wasn't stupid enough to try the wrong dance in the wrong territory.

I found a jean jacket with a beige top to match the faux-Timberland Nike boots I bought. At 130 dollars, I couldn't afford Timbs, but the 65-dollar Nike alternatives wouldn't be as mercilessly clowned as the Payless knockoffs.

At home, I readied myself. I didn't start wearing makeup until college, so getting ready literally consisted of taking a shower, lotioning[4] and deodorizing, putting on clothes, and taking my braids out of their ponytail. *Boom.* Dancing Queen ready.

My friend Monique's mom picked me up and my mother came out to our balcony to wish me off, calling, "Have fun, girls!"

I met Monique my first day of high school. As if I weren't already anxiously anticipating the first day of school, my mother accompanied me to the school bus stop at the Crenshaw and Slauson intersection. We stood next to the Kentucky Fried Chicken while I watched some of the older kids, also waiting for the bus, interact. As I checked out the scene, my mother recognized a parent who was waiting with her daughter. Thankfully, I wasn't the only lame girl whose mother deemed it necessary to accompany her to the 'hood bus stop. I pretended to be unfazed by the toothless, pee-pee-scented, drunk homeless woman with five blankets wrapped around her who was cursing out random strangers. *Don't let them sense your fear.* (Weeks later, I would find out her name was Peaches.) I focused instead on some of the upperclassmen guys, who looked like fine, grown men.

My mother, now surrounded by young women, called me over. "Jo-Issa, come over here!" She turned to the group of girls:

---

4 Black people of all shapes, sizes, and personalities value the moisturizing product known as body lotion. Lotioning alleviates ashiness. To be "ashy" is to be unkempt. Lotioning is the very least one can do to be socially presentable and physically acceptable. Cocoa butter, shea butter, and aloe vera are black-people essentials; some treat the moisturizing process as a meditative ritual. Some use only as much as necessary to cover the ashiest areas (knuckles, elbows, and knees). But all understand its importance.

"Have you ladies met my daughter, Jo-Issa?" *Of course they haven't, MOM!!!!*

The parent of one of the girls shook my hand as the other girls stared, and said politely, "No, hey." The girls introduced themselves to me as I nodded with embarrassment, and when the bus finally came, none of the girls sat next to me. That's where I met Monique, who still reminds me of that pitiful introduction.

I never would have imagined that a year later she'd be accompanying me to the Dance of Doom. She echoed everyone else's excitement to see me dance. I half-heartedly played along. "Yeah, I'm pumped."

Twenty minutes later (it *does* take at least twenty minutes to get anywhere in L.A.), we made it to the border of Carson and Compton, where Lakira resided. My butterflies kicked in as I stepped out of the car and waved good-bye to Monique's mom. We were led to the backyard, where a cluster of sophomores in jean outfits and bright colors bobbed to loud music. It was the nighttime version of Mack 10's "Backyard Boogie."

The absence of alcohol from my entire high school experience was both a blessing and a curse. A blessing because we managed to have fun, amazing bonding experiences *without* alcohol (which made the experiences I had in college *with* alcohol that much more special) and a curse because that means every embarrassing thing that I did was the result of being completely sober. That's a sad realization.

As Monique and I went around the outskirts of the party, acting as if we were excited to see people we had seen just the day before, my eye kept wandering to the patch of grass in the center that had been labeled the "dance floor." Optimistically, I thought I might actually get away with spending the entire evening socializing. The dance floor was empty and nobody was paying attention to me. If only I were so lucky. Out of nowhere, Maurice, one of the cutest guys in our class, approached Monique to dance. Her playful resistance caused a scene as he dragged her to the center and started working her, while people watched. All the "uh-oh's!" and "get 'em's!" caught Lakira's attention and brought her next to me as she watched the scene with glee. She turned to me. "You ready to get down? You next!"

On cue, having finished being humped by Maurice, Monique yelled out, "Get Jo! Get Jo!" The crowd still watching, Maurice shrugged and pulled me to the dance floor. Monique, Lakira, and the rest of my sophomore peers watched as Maurice moved behind me and Trina's nasally vocals serenaded us. I had to back up all the talk I had spewed in the last two weeks, and so I stiffly bent my knees, booty popped (or "back-popped," if I'm being honest), and swayed to the best of my ability. I heard laughter and general aloofness.

Determined to make an impression, I swung my braids back and dropped to the floor on all fours, arching my back in the literal bad-bitch position. My hands on the ground, pumping my butt to the beat, I heard the cheers, the gasps, and the laughter behind me. And then came the flash of cameras. My heart stopped. The flashes could only mean one thing—someone was going to capture this moment and share it with others to further humiliate me beyond this evening. Because what could be more humiliating than feeling compelled to get on all fours just to gain social credibility?

When the song was over, I got up, ashamed and mortified on the inside and yet boastful on the outside, as Maurice moved his humping elsewhere. Monique approached me dying of laughter. "I got that shit on camera, HAHAHAHA!"

I don't remember how long we stayed at the party, because I kept replaying that moment over and over again, wishing I could be teleported to the future when all was forgotten.

I was so afraid of what was to come. Relieved the party was over and that the truth was finally out there, I still had to deal with the consequences the following Monday. I started to think of the excuses I could give.

Maybe I could blame their inevitable lack of appreciation of my dance moves on cultural differences. "That's how we dance in Senegal. I was trying to put *you* on game," I could snap with much 'tude.

Or perhaps I could blame my moves on dizziness. "Y'all know I suffer from vertigo. That's why I had to get low."

I practiced my "take me seriously" face in the mirror as I prepared for school.

But when I got to class, my fears were never realized. Instead of being called out for not being able to dance, I became known as "that smart girl who dropped it to the floor at Lakira's party." People who went to the party only talked about how much fun they'd had, leaving people who hadn't made it to regret missing it. Not only had I made a huge deal about how my dancing would affect my social reputation, but I had also neglected to realize that a lot of my fellow students weren't even invited. My invite automatically made me cool! My moves didn't kill my rep; if anything, my antics only served to briefly boost Lakira's popularity as an excellent party thrower. All order was restored. I had paid my dues and completed my black-girl rite of passage. Recognizing this, and the anxiety this whole ordeal had caused me, I decided I never had to attend another high school dance party ever again. Not even prom. Now, whenever I'm peer pressured to show off my moves, I politely bow out, "I don't fit the stereotype."

# Hair Hierarchy

It took me a while to embrace my natural hair. Sure, it helps that natural hair is in now, but even before natural hair was all that, I had, after years of struggle, learned to appreciate the autonomous locks that rest atop my head.

I didn't always have a grievance with my hair. When I was younger, our love-hate relationship was 70/30, in favor of love. Hate entered the picture only when my mother would style my tender-headed scalp, rushing to comb my kinks out with a fine-tooth as we got ready for school. The hate should have been directed at my scalp for being so sensitive, but in my eyes, my insubordinate hair was to blame. I'd witnessed the white girls in my class manage their hair with ease, the comb flowing through it, as though slicing through water. Even the Jewish girls, whose hair was "white-girl curly," had Moses strands that seemed to part for the comb to pass. Why did my hair choose to be so difficult?

It didn't help that I had to sit on a West African woman's floor for six to ten hours at a stretch as she braided my hair for the convenience of my mother (and, as I grew up, for my own convenience). This long length of time would be bearable if *every damn West African woman* that took me on as a client didn't marathon the Lifetime Channel. If only the sensitivity and empathy these women shared with the overly dramatic characters on-screen translated to how they braided their client's hair as they twisted and pulled every inch of my scalp with their rapid-fire fingers. Still, until I went to high school and found out how important "edges" are to the black female community, the two to three months of hassle-free hair almost seemed worth the time and pain.

What love I did have for my hair stemmed from my elementary school—an environment that embraced difference. Being among an ethnically diverse group of friends was great for my self-esteem. I was celebrated for being different, for having superhero hair that defied gravity and recoiled with lightning-speed elasticity. My hair texture was the subject of awe, confusion, and probably envy. I *loved* it. The desire other kids had to touch my hair didn't bother me at all. Instead, I felt special. Original. Sure, their hair was easier to deal with, but everybody and their mom had that type of hair. I was different. And in elementary school, different meant "better." Part of my identity was tied to the uniqueness of my hair and I was proud of that.

Until I moved to Los Angeles.

Moving from a predominantly white elementary school where I had an abundance of like-minded friends to a predominantly black junior high in L.A. where I knew *no one* was already an eye-opening experience. But nobody prepared me for the "hair hierarchy."

If you don't understand how it works, the hair hierarchy rates worth by length and texture of hair. The longer, silkier, and more European your hair, the higher your worth. The shorter, kinkier, and more African your hair? Kill thyself.

I was taught this caste system by a trio of mean girls in middle school who found glee in taunting me. To them, my insistence on wearing my hair in an Afro puff made me an easy target. "Watch out for Jo-Issa," one girl mused, "she might take something out of her nappy hair and throw it at you." Middle school girls are cruel. Clever but cruel. Even now, almost twenty years later, I harbor resentment toward these girls, but I'm also impressed by how funny some of their quips were, as if they used middle school as their comedy lab. In fact, one girl is now an actress/comedian who actually reached out to me on Facebook a couple of years ago and asked to be a part of my web series, *The Misadventures of Awkward Black Girl*, when it started to gain popularity. I looked at my computer, thinking, *BITCH, ARE YOU KIDDING ME?!?!?!?! HAHAHAHAHAHAHAHAHAHAHHAAHHA! BOW DOWN TO THE NAPPY PRIESTESS, MUTHAF$#@&%!*

It wasn't just that I suddenly found myself in the company of mean girls. It was also that it was the mid-nineties, and styles were changing. Long, flowing hair was in and weaves, though still the butt of many jokes in the black community, were rapidly becoming the norm. And as my luck would have it, braids with burnt ends, a hairstyle I frequently donned, were *just* going out of style. Still, nothing could have prepared me for the hate and ridicule I'd receive for wearing my hair in its natural state. Despite whatever was trending, I couldn't understand why people were so concerned with how *my* hair looked when it grew out of *my* scalp. Why was it so offensive?

Of course, my sixth-grade brain didn't really know to ask those questions or fully understand the history and social implications of my natural hair, so I just handled it the best way I could—by hiding it. Over the course of my middle and high school years, I hid my hair through braids, scarves, thin, flat-iron presses, and hoods—anything just to avoid showing my real hair in public. My hair, once a source of confidence, became my burden of shame.

My mother was disgusted by my insecurity.

"Why do you keep covering your head?!" she would yell, frustrated.

"Because you married an African, MOM! AN AFRICAN!" I would cry-yell, *Full House* style, in my head (because I knew better).

She just didn't get it. For one thing, my mother was "light-skinned," and though she wore her hair naturally at times, her softer-looking texture differed from mine. Furthermore, she and my aunt, whose hair was that "good, silky Indian" hair, grew up during the sixties and seventies, when natural hair was a statement of pride and militant activism. The only source of judgment she faced was from my Southern grandparents, who couldn't fathom why their daughters wouldn't straighten their wild Afros. They didn't have to face throngs of straight-haired middle school girls, or endure the public shunning of cute high school guys. I mean, sure, they were ostracized and brutalized for their skin color in general, but tomato/tomahto. My mother didn't know *my* struggle.

I begged her to let me relax my hair like the other girls at my school. In fact, it was at the suggestion of some of my black girl-friend allies that I got a perm. My mother warned me repeatedly that my hair was too soft to handle the chemicals in a relaxer, but I insisted. Perhaps my pleading eyes moved her to let me do it. A few weeks after rocking my fresh relaxer, I noticed that my hair started to break off at rapid speed. I tried to defend my jagged, rough edges to my friends at school.

"Dang, your hair is so short," one girl snapped.

"That's 'cause I had cut it . . ." I lied, as I twirled a strand that came off on my finger.

After the deed was done and my hair fell out, I'm pretty convinced that my mother just wanted to say, "I told your bald-headed ass so."

I soon realized that I was worse off than when I started. The sad fact that I was willing to damage my own God-given hair before wearing it out in public was not lost on me. By college, I knew that I had deep-rooted hair issues and sought to come to terms with it by experimenting with natural hairstyles. But when I went home to show off my twisted locks, my little brother was quick to tell me that, aesthetically, my hair "didn't look right."

After college, I moved to New York and started experimenting with weaves. It was like cheating. I could achieve the coveted top tier of the "hairarchy" while keeping my natural hair hidden underneath. Still, the difference in reception to "my" new hair was astonishing. Guys who had never and would never talk to me before were suddenly attentive and girls wanted to befriend me. Having a weave even inspired me to start dressing differently and carrying myself more confidently. Still, the disrespect to my former kinks was blatant.

When I moved back to Los Angeles and reunited with my friends, they too were impressed with my new New York look. "Girl, you look fly!" Even my younger brother who had dismissed my college twists paid me a compliment, the first *ever*, directed at my physical self. "Wow, your hair looks nice," he said, as he opened the door to let me in.

A mere change of styles was changing my life socially and opening all kinds of doors that had previously been shut. I became hip to the life in which I had been so desperate to participate.

It lasted but a moment. One evening, while unraveling my weave, I noticed the damage done to my actual hair. Not only was my hair thinning from all the under-weave braiding, but I also had about nine different textures going on in my hair at the same time— curly patches, dry patches, straight patches, thin patches, long patches, short patches. My hair was having an identity crisis! And *that* was the last straw for me. Who was I trying to fool?

*Oh, him.* I had started dating the man of my dreams back when I had braids. He had been begging to see my "real" hair for some time. Black men, I discovered, are just as obsessed with hair as black women are. His dating history included various ethnicities, many of whose hair could have been packaged and put on the shelf at a Korean beauty salon. That silky shit.

In a flashback to my middle school days, I was worried that by revealing my hair texture, I would drive him away or somehow make him appreciate me less. Having listened to many of my male friends express their desire for girls with long, flowy or curly hair, I determined that my hair was not desirable, which made me insecure. If I were to wear my natural hair around my new beau, I'd be vulnerable, at the mercy of his distaste. I wasn't ready for that yet. So, I passed off my weaves as my real hair. He seemed happily unaware. When I finally decided to stop pretending and show him my true texture, I realized I couldn't. My hair was damaged and uncooperative.

Then one day when I was in a music-video-watching mood I saw that Natalie Stewart (of Floetry fame) had released a new solo music video. In it, she was bald. And she looked *stunning*. Beautiful. Gorgeous. But most of all, she seemed so free. I had seen plenty of bald women before, but for reasons I can't explain, her look made the deepest impression on me at a time when I was already frustrated with the hold my hair had on my identity. If only I could do the same.

I first expressed my desire to cut off all my hair via Facebook. The response was all but encouraging.

"But what if you have a lumpy shaped head?"

"HAHAHAH you're gonna look so busted!"

"Don't do iiiiiiit!"

"OMG, if you do, take pictures!"

With so many strong opinions, the stubborn girl in me was insistent on going through with it. However, before I made my decision, I briefly discussed it with my boyfriend.

"I'm thinking about cutting my hair," I told him over the phone.

"Why?"

"Because I'm tired of it. I want to start over and grow it out again."

"I don't think you should do it."

He changed the subject to something else, but I had already made up my mind. Two weeks later, on a crisp October Friday evening, I drove myself to the salon down the street and walked in.

"Hey, is your barber in today?" I asked upon entering.

"Yeah, but he's backed up. Whatchu want done?" the receptionist asked, her back turned to me.

"I want to cut off all my hair."

She turned around. "You want to go bald?"

"Yes."

"You going through some *Waiting to Exhale* shit?"

"No. I just want to start over."

"Okay. Go see Keith over there."

I sat down next to three men, who were also waiting as Keith lined up a customer. Recognizing that this was going to take a while, I texted two of my dearest friends.

**ME:** I'm doing it. I'm at the barber now.
**JEROME:** Nuh-unh! I just got off, I'm coming.
**DEVIN:** Me too!

My friends joined me within the hour and stayed with me as I sat, bursting with excitement and anticipation. Two hours later, Keith was ready for me.

"So you just want me to cut it off?" he asked, unfazed.

"Yes. All of it."

"Cool."

And with that, he swiftly took the cutters to the front of my head. *Bzzzzzz.* As he started to George Jefferson me, I watched my locks fall down to the ground with a brief moment of panic. Was I doing the right thing? I could stop now and just wear a hat for months. But before I could complete the thought, half my hair was gone. It was time for me to accept my decision. I watched my friends' eyes for any sign of horror; none so far. When it was over, the ladies in the salon and the barber all looked on with smiles.

"Wow, bald looks good on you."

"For real. You got a cute-shaped head. Not a lot of women can pull that off."

I turned to my friends.

"It actually looks . . . beautiful," said Devin.

"You look gorgeous. Not gonna lie—I thought you'd look ugly as $#&%. But, wow," Jerome marveled.

I smiled and held the mirror up. There I was.

Initially, I'd decided to cut all my hair off as a way to start over *and* to take a break from the stress that my hair was causing me. Yet in doing so, I found it liberated me in ways I could never imagine. Not only was it a lazy person's idea of heaven, but having no hair showed me how stupid and trivial my insecurities about hair were. Where Samson found strength in his locks, I shed them to find mine. It was one of the best, most life-affirming decisions I've ever made.

Now, my hair and I are best friends. We've formed a new relationship and a mutual respect for each other. I'm learning to take care of her and am no longer afraid to introduce her to my friends. It's the most wonderful feeling in the world to be comfortable in my own healthy hair. Though my boyfriend initially hated my bald head, the sixth-grade me would be pleased to know that, contrary to what those middle school bitches thought, he appreciates me as I am.

# ABG Guide: The Hair Advantage

For the masses, the hair of the Awkward Black Girl (and even Boy) is an enigma. Though not generally known, NASA is even examining strands of our hair for space research, as its gravity-defying properties are key to missing answers in the field of aeronautics. Its buoyancy and ability to shrink when exposed to water is also rumored to be studied by scientists interested in underwater living.

It's not just appealing to science; entrepreneurs see opportunity too. Every day more and more products appear to cater to the diverse spectrum of our hair. Each new product claims the ability to tame our hair in a way that other manufacturers don't understand. Subscription boxes, forums, online videos, community meet-ups, and conferences are all dedicated to the mastery of hair. It's a billion-dollar industry.

For the Awkward Black Girl, it is important to view hair as the ultimate form of expression, an opportunity to be noticed and/or to be understood. Complete strangers can become allies or even friends due to respect for each other's hair. This can be positively promising. But there remains a sensitivity with our hair when others express unwarranted opinions and questions.

Even within the black community, hair adjectives like *laid*, *fried*, *nappy*, *jacked*, *whipped*, *dry*, and *snatched* are all used to convey approval or disapproval. They are used judgmentally, as if they assess not just hair but also character, quality of life, and decision-making skills. When dealing with people who pose so-called questions even as they judge you, here are some foolproof responses.

**Question:** "Is it real?"

Thanks to the widespread popularity of hair extensions, this question is no longer asked solely within the black community. Some people are even desensitized to the question. For those who aren't, the proper response is usually, "Is yours?" with a smile. If that person does not relent, you can try, "It's as real as you are bold," with a friendly chuckle. Passive aggression is absolutely appropriate in this instance. (Equal offenders: *Is it yours? How long is your actual hair?*)

**Opinion:** "It's so soft. I wasn't expecting that."

A backhanded compliment I receive often, it always begs the silently self-posed question, "What exactly were you expecting? Did you expect it to prick you like cotton plants, or to feel rough like gauze tape?" This usually comes from friends I've let touch it, or whom I've asked to braid my hair, or from chatty hairstylists. The only response I've been able to muster is a curt, "I know, isn't it?"

**Question:** "Can I touch it?"

The dreaded question that many with "ethnically expansive" hair have heard countless times. A simple, "Are your hands clean?" not only infantilizes the request, but it also sends the message that your hair isn't the sheep exhibit at the petting zoo. Should you decide to decline the request, a polite "I'd rather you not" should do the trick. If you see that the asker's spirit is crushed, and you're inclined to care, simply qualify your denial with, "I'm *very* tender-headed."

**Opinion:** "You should press it."

This opinion is almost always unsolicited. It is an opinion most commonly held by the older generation in the South where, in certain parts, natural hair is meant to be hidden, not seen. So as not to cause confusion or uproar, a simple "Maybe" or "One day" is enough to give them the hope that you'll gain some sense and "do something with that hair."

**Question:** "How did you get your hair like that?"

If the question's context refers to a complicated hairstyle, i.e. gravity-defying twists or an insanely thick side bun, this question is acceptable. If this question refers to one's hair texture, i.e. "Can I make my hair 'nappy' like yours?" or "Why doesn't my hair shrink when water touches it?" then we have a problem. Because "kinkify it" is not a readily available option in the hair salon, those whose scalps don't naturally produce such awe-inducing tresses may be confused or uninformed. So as not to exhaust oneself by explaining genetics, an appropriate response would be, "I woke up like this."

**Opinion:** "I wish my hair did that."

Ah, hair envy. There is no proper response to appease those who can't achieve the nap-tural roots. But this admission, especially given the self-esteem-threatening history of "nappy" rejection, is always appreciated. An appropriate response is, "Thanks."

---

By the year 2100, when the world is even more globally connected, with intergalactic travel common and interracial mixing the default, we can expect less of a fascination with the mystery of "black" hair. Until then, during your lifelong hair journey, understand that many will want to touch your hair and some will. A number will speculate on its authenticity; few will care. Consistency is boring. Variety is key. Don't be afraid to try various styles and numerous textures, with confidence. Proudly exclaim, *"I can wear my hair however I want, whenever I want, anywhere I want!"* The advantages of black hair are infinite.

# Public Displays of Affection

While I was scrolling through Twitter, I came across this picture on Instagram that a ponytail-wearing, plaid-shirt-donning, braces-wielding teenage girl posted. In it, she smiled happily in the mirror, her room adorned with all the generic decorations that fourteen-year-old girls fancy. She lay on her bed, stomach down, elbows propped up, to pose for her picture. At the foot of the bed, directly behind her, stood her bare bird-chested, undergarmentless, curly-high-top teenage boyfriend. His penis wasn't visible because, well, because they were *doing* it.

Kids, these days—gotta love 'em.

As social media redefines the boundaries of privacy, and the term "public" expands to limits that I can't even fathom, one thing remains the same: *I don't EVER want to see you and your significant other's displays of affection.*

PDA used to be more or less avoidable. As in, I could just turn my head and walk in the other direction or leave the dinner that we agreed would be just the two of us, to which you brought your new girlfriend with whom you keep making out. But since a relationship isn't officially recognized by the public these days without an incessant display of a couple's inseparability, here we are. And it's gross. And inconsiderate.

According to my mother, when I was a toddler I used to love PDA. Whenever I'd see two characters on-screen kissing, I would exclaim, "Look, Mommy, they're married!" Had I employed the same prudish logic in my teenage years, maybe I would have surmised that my parents' marriage wasn't doing so well. They never kissed in front of us. Or said "I love you" in front of us. In fact, the words "I love you" were reserved for life-threatening occasions (i.e. air travel and accidents) and birthday-card signatures. There was no doubt in our minds that our parents loved each other, but if I were to evaluate my parents' love based on their PDA, I'd think they were just above an arranged marriage.

My parents had other ways of showing their affection without openly fondling each other. They joked frequently and often made each other laugh. I think my mom made my dad laugh more, which I loved. Even now, our sense of humor is what binds us as a family. It's how we express love. It's the reason that I sit at the kitchen table for hours at a time when my four siblings are in town and just laugh and laugh. I don't know that I've ever told any of my siblings that I love them, but if anything, my tearful laughter expresses that emotion on my behalf.

Perhaps it's because I've found other ways to say "I love you" *without* saying those exact words that I have trouble saying it now. The words seem so unnecessarily dramatic. I would much rather be shown love than to merely hear the words. Not everyone agrees; some people won't know it's love until the expression of it is so obvious and public it's displayed on Facebook. *Really?* If you ask me, your unctuous displays of love should be kept to your damn self.

Growing up, the words "I love you" were a special gift, from me to you. I didn't say it often and when I said it, I absolutely meant it. It was for you and only you at the specific time that I chose to utter it. Then I went to private school in Brentwood and befriended a bunch of white girlfriends who dished out those words as if they were meaningless.

"Ohmygodiloveyou."

"I love you, you're the best."

"Can I just say that I love you?"

I would always just laugh it off, unsure of what to say in return, worried about being insincere. I watched as those words turned into public caressing and hand-holding and kissing and groping. It was almost as if they were checking to see if anyone was watching, hoping they were watching. Mini, preteen exhibitionists.

The first time I was both intrigued and repulsed by PDA was when my younger siblings and I took a trip with my parents to Paris. We were visiting my Tonton Bocar's family and sightseeing. As we walked through some famous Parisian park that I couldn't have cared less about—because I was ten and tired of walking and developing what would become a lifelong hatred for tourism—I spotted a couple on the open lawn, going *at* it. They were laid out on a blanket as the man kissed the woman's neck and started to disrobe her. She stroked his back, her eyes thrilled and ecstatic. Then as I walk-watched, I swear I noticed her check to see if anyone was watching. Like, "Look at me and my adventurous sexual relationship. Look at ME, EVERY-BODY!" And *that*, more than the public act of doing it in a park full of kids, was what disturbed and annoyed me most. How dare she?

PDA signals a desperate need for outside validation of one's relationship status. "Look at how he kisses me in front of you all. Surely he loves me. Don't you wish you had this?"

How ironic, then, that my very first kiss was a public display of affection. Well, not really "affection," so much as "acquaintance." A shameful display of acquaintance. I don't know how it happened, but I was so proud of myself at the time. I felt so validated. It was the summer after sixth grade. My mother had decided that the school I was attending, Palms Middle School, wasn't enough of a challenge for me. Not only that, but my sixth-grade best friend Ashley's mother had decided to enroll her in a private school. When Ashley was pulled out of Palms, I was, too. The entire process was just like applying for college, I'd find out later. My mother set up appointments for me at the top private schools, Harvard-Westlake, Windward, Archer, Crossroads, and Brentwood. Once there, I'd interview with the headmasters and charm them with my intellect and vast and worldly twelve-year-old experience. Then I'd go back to sixth grade and sit in class, fantasizing about my new, diverse, state-of-the-art future.

Much to my delight, I got accepted into all of the schools. I couldn't decide between Harvard-Westlake and Brentwood. But I remember that during my Brentwood tour a really cute (probably not, I had horrible sixth-grade taste), white, brown-haired upperclassman waved to me as he leaned coolly on his desk, a pencil in his mouth. That image of coolness and the potential for diverse love interests solidified my choice of Brentwood.

But my mother had toured the schools along with me, and in her eyes there were very few black faces in what seemed like an overbearing sea of white. She feared that my sense of identity would be snuffed out and needed reassurance that I'd be okay. She discussed it with Ashley's mother and discovered ABC. An acronym for A Better Chance, ABC was headed by a short but robust, shiny-scalped black man named Michael who served as the preemptive olive branch between black kids and the private school system. The organization was founded to make sure we didn't get lost in the private school culture, that kids with less fortunate economic backgrounds or kids who were prone to forget that they were black or Latino would always have a place to simultaneously uplift and ground them. This was music to my mother's ears.

What excited me the most was that there was an ABC summer retreat, right before I would begin junior high in the fall. A *co-ed* retreat in Northern California?! What a perfect opportunity to find a boyfriend! This was a must for me. Ashley and I prepared, giddy with opportunity.

Except that everyone hated me. With the exception of one girl—who hailed from Inglewood, loved chicken nuggets, and was dubbed "Cheerful Cherie" for her upbeat attitude—nobody thought I was cool. My "uncool" status was established on the bus ride we took up to the Bay. My mother insisted that she, my little brother (nine), and my little sister (six) would ride with us and take a return flight home. Aside from the designated chaperone, she was the *only* parent present. But since my mother was gracious enough not to sit near me so as to fully embarrass me, no one besides Ashley knew that the family in the back belonged to me.

The trip started off hopeful enough. Ashley and I watched as various junior high schoolers of all shapes and sizes and both genders filled the bus. That's when I saw him for the first time. I tried not to stare as he walked onto the bus. Taller than me, crème-brûlée-colored skin, green eyes, puberty buff—it was lust at first sight. I jabbed Ashley with my elbow.

"Ohmygod, he's SO fine."

"Who?"

"Don't look, but he's about to walk past us. Don't look don't look."

Ashley looked.

"Him? He's not fine. He's cute."

He walked to the back of the bus. *This is going to be so much fun,* I thought.

Then my little sister got stuck in the bus bathroom and lost. her. MIND. My little sister who grew up to be a cool, calm, and collected germophobe *freaked out* at the thought of being stuck in the bus bathroom. She started banging on the door, yelling, "I CAN'T GET OUT, MOM! I CAN'T GET OUT!" To which my mother rushed to help her baby girl, while everyone on the bus turned in their direction. When my mother failed to get through to her, assuming I'd know more about bus engineering, she called me.

"Jo-Issa, help your sister! Jo-Issa!"

Ashley fell out laughing as I sunk in my seat, pretending that my name was anything but that which my mother shrieked. Thankfully, one of the young fine gentlemen sitting near the back came to my sister's rescue and simply and calmly told her to try *turning the knob to the left.* And, presto, the door opened. My sister emerged, with tear-stained eyes, grateful to be let free from the grip of the bathroom monster (a level-one boss, at best). I remained in my seat, mortified.

By the time we arrived at Mills College, an all-girls campus, the color had returned to my face and my hope for the trip had been restored. The campus was beautiful, and I felt like I had fast-forwarded to the college chapter in my life. We got off the bus and I looked up at what must have been the most beautiful dorms on campus, akin to freshly renovated, quaint townhomes. As Ashley and I made our way toward them, we heard hand claps.

"All right, guys, those are the residence halls for college students," Michael said. "You guys will be staying over there."

Our heads turned collectively as he pointed to what looked like a haunted, abandoned part of campus that we hadn't even noticed before. It looked as if it had just emerged from the depths of hell. Ghosts of students past were wailing and circling the dilapidated roofs and breathing fire on the tattered exterior. The disappointment was palpable.

Michael remained cheery. "This is where the international students stay. Make friends! Learn a language!"

One of the girls we stood next to shook her head. "Dag. They get the Holiday Inn and we get the Motel 6." I cracked up laughing. Later, upon recalling this memory, I laughed again at how our frame of reference for "luxury" was the Holiday Inn. The hotel/motel girl introduced herself as Kim. With caramel skin and her hair in a sock bun, which accentuated her beautiful cheekbones, she was tall, thin, and pretty. Next to her stood a girl who had African-American facial features but looked closer to white. She introduced herself in a thick East Coast accent as Taipei. With long, jet-black hair that she wore partially up, she was Italian and black (clearly a mix more common than I thought; see "A/S/L"). She had a cute gap between her teeth that actually looked good on her (I had a gap between my teeth that I hated, mostly because my little brother and sister would parody the Gap theme song with, "Fallllll into Jo-Issa's gap!"). The most notable thing about her was that she was a lesbian, and I had never met one up until that point. She was edgy and cool. Both Taipei and Kim were fourteen, going into high school.

My best friend, Ashley, who I clutched onto as if for (social) life, was the *only* reason I was able to get in with these cool girls. With her long hair, cocoa skin, puberty boobs, and "chinky" eyes, Ashley was constantly approached by boys and adored by girls alike. And that girl could dance. She was everything I wasn't and, as such, she fit in perfectly with the cool girls, despite being two years younger than they were. When our families were first introduced, we discovered that she and I were distant cousins, by marriage. To deepen our bond and solidify the potential for coolness in my own genes, I publicly identified her as my cousin.

As we unpacked our belongings in our respective hostel rooms, we were also introduced to Jennifer, a pretty, petite girl with an infectious high-pitched squeal-laugh, who went to elementary school with Cheerful Cherie. They would both be attending Brentwood, the same private school as me. Up until that point, I hadn't met anyone else who would be joining me at Brentwood, so I tried to stay close to them. Jennifer was hesitant, but Cherie welcomed me with open arms.

We all gathered together in Kim and Taipei's room to discuss the program, our schools, and of course, *boys*. We talked about who was cute, who was checking for whom, and our personal relationship statuses. Before I could mention my crush, Taipei spoke up. "That boy with the green eyes is really cute. I think his name's Jordan." *Trick, what?! Don't you like girls?*

Ashley and I exchanged glances as I nodded silently.

"Jo-Issa likes him, too," she blurted.

Taipei turned to me. "He's cute, isn't he?"

"Yeah, he is fine. He's a fine *boy*," I confirmed.

"He's Italian and black, just like me. Small world."

*Small-ass world, in-fucking-deed. Too small for lesbians to be claiming the most attractive boys at our haunted college, too. But, whatever.* Then it was only a matter of time (hours, even) before the two of them were booed up. That night, at one of our first mixers, they hit it off and started making out. All week. She had won him, and I dismissed the idea of ever having a chance with him.

The rest of the retreat was unmemorable, until the final dance. It was a semi-formal, but the closest thing I had to that was business casual—my brand of awkward involves fashion faux pas. I wore a long black skirt with a white collared short-sleeve top. *Boom*: semi-formal. I had flashbacks to my sixth-grade dance the year before—where dateless and rhythmless, I wandered about by myself—and decided not to get my hopes up this time around. Ashley was my "date," but that didn't mean much as she was constantly being asked to dance, left and right, leaving me to wander as if I were looking for someone in the glass-door ballroom's completely open space.

Kim, Jennifer, and Cherie were dancing in a group on the dance floor, so I joined them. But Taipei was missing.

"Where's Taipei?" I asked Kim.

"She's on the phone in her room. I think she's breaking up with her girlfriend."

*Girlfriend?* I remembered Ashley mentioning that Taipei's phone was constantly blowing up but neglected to put two and two together. She had been cheating on her girlfriend with Jordan this entire time. I looked around the party with actual purpose this time. Jordan was on the dance floor having a good time, dancing with girls here and there, but for the most part, he was by himself.

I didn't have the besties-before-testes, sisters-before-misters values and morals that I hold so strongly to today. Instead, I slowly and nonchalantly started to two-step drift toward him, my butt poked out, until I made contact. He smiled and we began freak-dancing. As we freak-danced to countless songs, the rest of the party disappeared. It was like the school dance scene where Tony and Maria first meet in *West Side Story*, except set to the rapper

Luke's soundtrack. As we danced face-to-face, he whisper-yelled a question in my ear.

"Do you want to go outside?"

"Yeah," I nodded.

My heart raced. What were we going to talk about? Had he appreciated my seductive grinding so much that he wanted to break up with Taipei? It would be a first but it was within reason, as Jordan wasn't the best dancer either. Ashley poked fun at how offbeat his pelvic thrusting was, but I didn't care; if anything, that endeared him to me even more.

He held my hand and led me outside. We were so close and I was so nervous, I don't even recall what kind of small talk we made. I do remember him leaning in to kiss me, and me kissing him back. It was my first kiss, much less my first tongue kiss, but I was ready and it was magical. I felt like the nerdy heroine in my own romantic comedy. I got the guy!

After minutes of making out, we went back inside to the party. My face glowing with excitement, I couldn't wait to break the news to Ashley. As I made my way back to the dance, behind Jordan, I was stopped by Michael, the head of the program. His demeanor was serious as he pulled me to the side in his slim-fitted, tiny suit. I stood guiltily as he mustered a friendly, guidance-counselor smile.

"Be discreet with your actions," he started.

"What do you—"

"Hhhhh-tuh-tuh-tuh-tuh!!!" He held his long index finger up and repeated, "Be discreet with your actions. Keep your business private." He then dismissed me. I was embarrassed, but still on a high from my first kiss. I told Ashley everything and she cracked up.

"Did he really 'hhhh-tuh-tuh-tuh' you?"

Other than Ashley, I kept my exchange with Jordan discreet from the other girls.

The next day, on the bus ride home, I sat with Cherie, sharing her Walkman and sneaking backward glances as Jordan and Taipei made out in the back. Why couldn't they be discreet? I wasn't mad or hurt, only relieved that Taipei didn't find out about me and Jordan. Once the magic of my first kiss faded away, I realized how stupid of me it was to kiss him in front of everyone, outside or not.

Months later, Ashley and I went to catch a matinee at Magic Johnson Theatres at the Crenshaw Mall. As we were making our way out, we saw Jordan and Taipei coming in. As Jordan stood by the door, avoiding my eye contact, Taipei came over and said, "Hi." My stomach clenched as I wondered whether or not he had told her about our kiss. She directed most of the conversation to Ashley and then gave me a snide smile as she walked away. It could have been my imagination, but I sensed that she knew and wasn't threatened. I may have had him once, but she had him all the time.

———

I wish I could say I had learned my lesson, but my exhibitionism didn't stop there. Years later, when I revisited my first love in Dakar, Senegal, to stay with my father's side of the family, my careless PDA almost got me in serious trouble. One night I convinced my older cousins to accompany me to the club where I first met my first boyfriend, Moise. Club Niani had become super popular since the time we went the year before. Now it was a tourist hub, full of teens. Still, none of that mattered to me. I was excited to be reunited with Moise (more on him in "Halfrican") and his friends. We had been corresponding via email for a year now and I was so happy they'd be joining us.

He arrived, dressed in his best American gear. We danced for an hour as my cousins sat down, bored, clearly doing me a favor. The club was getting packed, sweaty, and hot. He asked if I wanted to go get some air outside. I got a bout of déjà vu and thought about Jordan asking me the same question years earlier. We walked up the steep flight of stairs that led to the club's exit. I looked around for my cousins. Not wanting them to follow me, I'd told them I was going to get some air outside really quickly. After Moise spoke to the bouncer in Wolof, ensuring we'd be able to get back inside, we left the club. It was so much quieter outside. We found an even more isolated spot and started kissing. Surely, this was a step up from kissing outside in front of a glass-doored ballroom.

Unfortunately, that wasn't the case. Just as I started getting teenage bold, playfully grabbing his butt, a military Jeep rolled up, honked, and shone its lights on us. Surprised and frightened, I quickly dropped my hands. Moise placed his hands in front of me, attempting to shield me from what he surmised would occur. Both soldiers exited the Jeep with urgency, long rifles strapped to their backs.

"*Lan le?*" Moise tried to ask in Wolof, a sign of informality. The police weren't having that. They spoke in French.

"*Qu'est-ce que vous faites?*" they asked.

"*On parle. Il faisait chaud en bas.*"

"*Vous faisiez plus que parler, viens avec nous.*" The soldier demanded that we go with him. Moise shook his head. I spoke up in my worst French accent.

"*Monsieur . . . qu'est-ce qu'on a fait? Je ne viens pas d'ici. Je suis Americaine.*"

"*Madame, vous s'embrasser en public. Nous faisons pas ça ici. Donc, je vais vous amener en prison.*"

"Prison?!" I shrieked.

Moise tried again. "*On savait pas, s'il vous plait.*"

The soldier stood there and waited. Moise nodded. Panic in my eyes, I told him I couldn't go to jail. Not only did my cousins not know where I was, but this trip already didn't have the same ease as last year's trip because my mother had joined us. My sense was that she had come to spy on me, having heard about Moise last year from one of my aunts. I had to sneakily plan club excursions to see him since he couldn't come by the house, as I didn't want her to embarrass me by asking him multiple questions or banning me from seeing him. Going to jail would not only reveal that I had gone to see him, but it would also infuriate and humiliate her and my family.

Moise reassured me in French. "They're not going to take us to jail. They just want money. I have some. Just pretend like you're giving me some money, too."

I nodded, furious but relieved. They were harassing us. *Stupid corrupt-ass military.* Moise turned back to the soldiers and gave them at least forty dollars.

"*C'est tous qu'on à.*" He insisted that was all we had.

The main soldier nodded his head. "*C'est bon, vas y.*"

He signaled for us to go back inside. We thanked him and went back in the club. Moise apologized, pissed off and embarrassed. I started laughing. It was my first taste of corruption and I was astonished that it could affect me personally. I rejoined my cousins, as if nothing had happened, resolving that my intimate moments were best left private.

# African Dad

**ME:** Hey, Dad! Are you free Sunday? We want to take you out to dinner.

I pressed "send" and placed my phone on my cubicle desk beside me, prepared to wait a lengthy while for a response. It was eleven o'clock in the morning; he was busy making his hospital rounds.

I went back to my assigned task of making calls to companies we had partnered with in years past, gauging their interest in active charitable giving the next year. Employed by the March of Dimes for six months now, I was feeling adjusted but anxious. My boss valued me and my promotion potential was fairly certain. However, my web series, *The Misadventures of Awkward Black Girl*, was gaining traction, and I was feeling claustrophobic as my window of opportunity to pursue my passion full-time was closing.

Scrolling the ten-page, double-sided list of Citibank branches,

I saw that I had completed only ten calls so far and they were all hesitant to commit. I hated this part of the job. How persistent could I be when my heart wasn't into it? We were working for a great cause, helping babies—but those babies didn't need me, specifically, in their corner.

My phone flashed. *That was fast.*

**DAD:** Ok! What for?

I smiled and shook my head. My dad barely remembered his own birthday, so this wasn't a surprise.

**ME:** For Father's Day! :-)
**DAD:** Oh! Lucky me. Can I bring my new wife? She wears blue wigs and has long colorful nails.

I held my phone in my hand closely and reread the message. I was amused, at first. What a strange joke! As far as I knew, my dad was still in a relationship with a woman I hated. He was very well aware of my ill feelings, so why would he joke about that? I knew he couldn't have married *her* ass, so that wasn't my worry.

My younger brother would know. He had been living with my father since his senior year of high school and always had the inside scoop, when he cared enough to pay attention.

"Hello." His voice was deep with a grogginess that should have been reserved for the early morning, as opposed to the early afternoon.

"Hey, is Dad high? I just sent him a text about Father's Day plans and he asked if he could bring his new blue-haired wife."

My brother's voice woke up. "Dude! I meant to tell you—Dad, like, had a conversation with me and basically said he's getting old and needs someone to take care of him. He told me he met someone and . . . I think he got married to this new lady."

I couldn't find my breath. *What the entire hell?* How had my dad gotten married a) without his family present and b) without so much as mentioning it to all of us? While on the one hand I tried to be offended, on the other hand, I was grateful that he had apparently moved on from the horrible woman who had caused my family so much pain and anger.

"Does Mom know?" I managed.

"I doubt it."

What would she think? Had he told her?

Welcome to my enigma. I have no idea what's going on with my dad emotionally and I've always been curious. Sometimes frustratingly so. I have no doubt where his head is when it comes to our family's material needs. He's a master provider, a champion in that role. Despite occasionally protesting about something being "too expensive," he has always been more than willing to give his kids everything they need to succeed and then some. But of all the men I've known, my father is the most lovingly distant. He's affectionate in his own way. I've found myself staring at the "Love, Dad" sign-off in the various "You need to pay these parking tickets" notes left for me at his house or at the end of the automatic "I'm alive!" email notifications his boat system sends us when he's at sea. Yet I've never heard the words "I love you" come out of his mouth. Never hearing those words uttered to my mother or my siblings probably affected me in some way before, but only in writing about it now does it hit home. The truth is that I've long wanted more of a relationship with my father, though this wasn't always the case.

———

I initially blamed my mother for the end of my parents' relationship. During my junior year of high school, on an otherwise unmemorable day, they gathered me, my little brother, and my little sister in my dad's cramped home office and blindsided us with the news.

"Your dad and I have decided to get a divorce."

My mouth opened and I pulled my eyebrows down into a worried frown. The three of us sat shocked. My parents' lives as I knew them flashed before my eyes. I had never seen them so much as fight. They had just celebrated a twenty-year anniversary during one of our summers in Maryland. I remember my mother standing before a small crowd of family and friends in our living room, holding a plastic glass of sparkling apple cider, braggadociously telling the story of how my dad noticed her for the first time:

". . . I was at a party with friends and we were all in line for the food, and I remember he saw me and turned to his friend and starting speaking Wolof. I didn't know much Wolof, but I could make out some words. And all I heard was, 'somethingsomething-something *bakhna*!'" The Senegalese invitees laughed as my mother explained to the non-Wolof speakers that *bakhna* means "good." My dad laughed and exclaimed sheepishly, "I was talking about the food!" More laughter.

This was my parents' relationship as I knew it. Now, they stood before us, their somber faces staring at ours. I wished they were calling us to berate us for being lazy children. Not for this. Divorce never seemed like an option for us, for them. I stared at them both, blankly, unable to understand.

"Why?" we all asked in some variation. My younger brother started crying, incredulous.

"Cultural differences," my mother told us, tearing up. I looked to my father, who nodded in agreement, sadness in his eyes. Why weren't they comforting each other? Then they hit us with the gut punch.

"Your dad will be moving out of the house."

More tears. What the hell were they doing to us? They reiterated the same mantra that all decent divorcees tell their kids: "This has nothing to do with you. This doesn't change how much we love you. We are still your parents." But my dad looked so sad. All I could think about was how he'd be all by himself. I had always known my father to spend a lot of time in solitude, reading, working, fishing. But I also assumed that he found comfort in coming home to his wife and his kids at the end of the day. Who would he come home to now?

For nearly six years of my life, I used to be my dad's favorite girl. I was the *only* girl, but I translated this term of endearment to mean "favorite child," which led me to have very high self-esteem. He'd come home from work and my older brother, Malick, would come into my room ominously and say, "Dad wants you." Because of his tone, my trip to my father's room would be marked with fear. But then I'd see his warm, smiling face and realize my brother was just being a jealous jerk. At ten, he was too big to do the special task that would help my dad unwind after a long day.

"Can you walk on my back?" he'd ask as he lay down on his stomach and, on occasion, fell asleep. And I would, pretending his back was a mountainous excursion that needed precise balance. At the end of his makeshift massage, he'd affectionately send me on my way, saying, "That's why you're my favorite girl!"

Then, two weeks before my sixth birthday, my little sister, Elize, was born and my title was stripped from me. I looked at her, sleeping peacefully and prettily in her crib, and asked, "Dad, am I still your favorite girl?"

He laughed, "Of course you are. You're Favorite Girl Number One and she's Favorite Girl Number Two."

I was old enough to recognize that there could be only one real favorite. I would share my title with NO ONE!

No sooner than a week after the divorce announcement, my dad moved to a nice luxury apartment with a fancy fountain and a large amusement park-ish pool about fifteen minutes away from us. His favorite place in Los Angeles was Marina del Rey, where all the yachts were docked and where he frequently met up with his fishing club. Twice a month, the club would set sail on a large fishing boat and try their luck. My dad's proudest catch was a fifty-pound halibut that he and his club members wrestled with for hours.

His new apartment was conveniently two minutes away from the 90 freeway, which was a five-minute straight shot right to the marina. We had just started to get used to having my dad under the same roof as us, as he used to commute from California, where he had opened a practice, to our home in Maryland, and after just four years together, we were no longer a solid family unit. During my elementary school years, when people asked me why my dad didn't live with me, I proudly told them the truth. Now, if they ever asked, they would get the answer they expected—divorce—and I hated that. So I didn't tell any of my friends for years. I wasn't so much ashamed as just saddened and protective. It was my family and it was our business, and I didn't want people knowing about any of the dents in our familial unit because my family's bond, in addition to our large size, was always an inexplicable source of pride for me.

My younger siblings and I never really discussed it either. We felt the void of our father's absence and harbored an unspoken resentment against my mother for not trying hard enough to stay with him. Or at least, I did. I was aware that my mother was also going through menopause at the time of the divorce, but at seventeen I didn't fully comprehend the extra layer it added to her emotional state. I remember her crying a lot, and I remember attributing her crying to the hormonal issues she had warned us about prior. But I never actually took the time to consider that she was hurting deeply. In my mind, she had ended the relationship: she was feeling bad about it, as she should. I wasn't a soothing shoulder for her to cry on and now, with hindsight, I get regret pangs when I think of how I wasn't there for her in those initial stages.

In one instance, my brother, sister, and I came home from school to find that she was still at work. After a couple of hours passed, we grew hungry, and I called and asked her what we'd be having for dinner.

"There's lots of food in the fridge—fix something!"

"Ugh. Fine," I obliged, with much brattitude. The three of us decided we'd cook up some hamburgers. We made a whole big, messy activity of it. When my mother came home that evening, exhausted from the day, she barely stepped foot into the kitchen before we jokingly boasted, "We made our own hamburgers!"

My mother looked around the kitchen, at the mess we had left behind. Then, she paused and frowned at us and said, "You didn't make me any?"

As my mother stood there, I realized this hadn't even occurred to any of us to do. What was wrong with us?

"No . . . we—" I started.

"Never mind." My mother shook her head angrily, rushing to her room. I exchanged glances with my brother and sister and braced myself to go to her bedroom and apologize. There she sat on her bed, crying to herself, wiping her own tears. I hugged her tightly and apologized, coming to terms with the fact that she needed us just as much as we needed her.

Several months later, my siblings and I grew accustomed to and even began to take advantage of the weekend visits with our father. We'd spend the night at his apartment and then we'd wake up to McDonald's breakfast orders for us in the morning. After we happily wolfed down our meals on his television trays, he'd resurface with an offer for the day's plans. "Do you all want to go to the bookstore?"

We were always game. There were certain things my dad didn't bat an eye about spending his hard-earned money on for his children: education, books, Senegal, and technology. In that order.

"Hey Dad, can I get money to go to the movies?"

"No. You don't need it."

"Hey Dad, can we go to Senegal?"

"Sure!"

We could always count on an unlimited budget for books and would spend at least an hour at the bookstore, each making our deliberate selections (sometimes reading them, in the store, before we purchased them only to read them again). Then we'd go home, go to our separate corners, and disappear into our individual worlds. That was how we bonded.

Whether out of guilt or his yearning for a new car, my dad left me with his 1997 Saturn. So when the provisional part of my license expired, my teen angst was freed and I was at liberty to visit my dad, my friends, and my new boyfriend. I chose the latter two far more often, but during one particular weekend, I decided I wanted to pay a visit to my younger cousin, Aida, and gossip about some boys in Senegal. She and her mother had just come in from Senegal and were staying with my father in his two-bedroom apartment.

My father had always made it abundantly clear that we were always welcome in his home, so I didn't feel the need to announce my visit to him beforehand.

I knocked on the door and Aida answered, surprised to see me. "Oh, hey, Jo-Issa."

"Hey, girl!" I stood in the doorway and saw my dad sitting at the bar, facing the kitchen, where my aunt Mame Aissa was cooking. Behind them, in the back of the room, I saw a woman I didn't recognize standing near the balcony door, talking on the phone. She looked in my direction and then held the phone closely to her mouth, uttering the words, "Oh my God." Not in the frightened sense, but in the "shit is about to go down" sense. Then she walked out onto the balcony and continued her phone call. There was a look of knowingness in Aida's eyes that disturbed me, like she was searching me for recognition or understanding of some sort.

This all happened within the span of four seconds, and it would take another couple of hours before I fully processed the scene before me. What struck me as immediately odd, however, was that my father, though pleasant, greeted me with, "Heyyy! You don't call?" His tone suggested a joke, but his stiff demeanor said the opposite. I looked to my aunt, who had the same searching eyes as my cousin. Something was going on. For the first time, I felt unwelcome in my own father's home.

Pretending to laugh at my dad's rhetorical accusation, I remained standing in the doorway. I told them I had just come by to talk to Aida. My dad, most likely finally sensing how awkward I felt, waved his hand and said, "Come in." But it was too late. I already felt like unwanted company. I shook my head, smiling.

"What did you want to talk to me about?" Aida asked me. To

maintain airs, I told her, "It's gossip. I'll just call you and tell you later."

"Are you sure?" she asked.

"Yeah," I said as I backed away, looking one last time toward the balcony, where the stranger whose presence eclipsed my comfort snuck glances. Then I said good-bye to everyone and left, my mind racing and replaying the moment the door opened, over and over again.

When I got home, my mother was undressing in her room. I knocked on her door. "Mom, are you busy?"

"Just a second!"

I considered how I was going to present my findings to her. I didn't want to be wrong in my assumption that dad had moved on so quickly, especially given her sensitive state. How would I tell her without hurting her feelings? But then, I remembered, she had been the one to end things, so maybe she wouldn't even bat an eye. Maybe she'd be happy for him. I was prepared to be, if she was. Either way, I needed to know what I had just experienced.

My mother slid her door open. "Yes, my sweetie?"

"Can I talk to you?" I asked. My mother's smile grew uneasy. Given my tone and her reaction, I'm pretty certain she assumed I was going to tell her I was pregnant or had HIV, so maybe my actual news would come as a relief. I sat down on her bed and she sat next to me, expectant.

"So, I just came from Dad's . . ."

Her shoulders relaxed slightly, but not much. "Yeah . . ."

I told her every detail of the story, including my cousin and aunt's reactions and the strange woman's ominous "Oh my God." I watched as my mother listened, taking my words in, processing them. Then I asked in a lighter tone, as though presenting her with what I was certain was an educated guess, a deduction at best, "Is Dad seeing someone new?"

My mom took a second, looking at me, contemplating. It was my turn to search her eyes, looking for a revelation of some sort, but I was also relieved not to be the bearer of any bad news when she nodded and said, "Unh-huh."

"Oh." *She did know*, I thought, exhaling, glad that was out of the way. As I revisited the scenario in my mind, something about the flashback and my mother's calm confirmation alarmed me. I could feel my heart pounding as the pieces started coming together. An overwhelming dread hit me and I gasped out loud. When I turned to my mother, she was already watching me, waiting.

"Is *that* why . . ."

My mother nodded, solemnly, before I could finish my question. It was as if she had transmitted her emotions to me. The tears came immediately, instantly, as though even *they* had been waiting for me to figure it all out. A sound escaped my throat that I didn't recognize as I bent into my lap and covered my face. *What? My dad?* Was my father even capable of this? How? Why? I felt my mother's arms around me, trying to hug the rock my body had become.

"I'm so sorry. I'm sorry, sugar . . ." she said softly.

"Who is she?" I managed to stammer through tears.

She shook her head. "She works at his office."

"What?! How long?" I had worked at his office for an entire summer when I was fourteen. Did I know her? Did she know me? How come I didn't recognize her face?

My mother rubbed my back. "I still don't know. I've been trying to find out."

"Do Amadou and Malick know?"

"Yes, I told them. But your father and I decided we didn't want you, Lamine, and Elize to have a bad image of him."

I started thinking about the image I had of my father and the deception I felt. He didn't even deserve my sympathy! All that time, I had been so concerned with him being alone, when my mother, my poor mother . . . I couldn't stop sobbing from the pain of the truth. I never would have imagined my peaceful, patient father could be capable of causing so much pain.

I stopped going to his apartment on weekends altogether, making excuses that were purposefully flimsy enough to make a statement, but sturdy enough to not tip off my younger brother and sister. I couldn't make conversation with him. I stopped asking him for things. I didn't want anything from him. If he noticed my distance, he didn't acknowledge it, which made me even angrier.

As far as my mother was concerned, my discovery had opened the floodgates of detail. As she pieced together the history of his affair, she learned how callous the woman he had chosen to involve himself with was. My mother had met her on very few occasions, but in every instance, she smiled in her face, while her actions spit on the past of which my mother had once been so certain. I had never hated anyone as much as I did her. I had never hated anyone, period. I'm never one to be bitchy for no reason. I actually sympathized with the stepmother in *The Parent Trap* (the Hayley Mills version), because I never thought the twins gave her a fair chance. And so, even after my discovery, I was prepared to give this other woman the benefit of the doubt. Maybe she didn't know. Maybe my father was a master deceiver and had been two-timing them both. Maybe she was remorseful, but too in love to back out? Maybe there was a justification for all of this hurt. But when I finally worked up the courage to ask my mother how and when she found out, I decided the other woman was undeserving of my empathy.

My one-sided rift with my father continued through my freshman year, slowly subsiding by the winter of my sophomore year with my decision to temporarily "stop out" of Stanford and take filmmaking classes at the New York Film Academy in Los Angeles. My decision required convincing both my parents, but especially my father, who was paying my tuition and who was not convinced that I would return. Convinced I was serious about my education and that he could count on me to still finish in four years, he felt a bit more at ease with my choice. After that, I decided that my anger toward my father required far more energy than I was willing to expend. I had to find a way to move on, especially since once I moved to Los Angeles for film school we'd be back in the same city for a while.

We didn't speak about *her* and I didn't bring *her* up again until my senior year, when I put on my fourth and final college production, a Motown adaptation of *Grease*. I invited all of my family living in Los Angeles up to see it, including my father. I heard through the family grapevine that my father was going to bring this woman up to my school to see my show. Aghast and indignant, I decided to write him a polite, respectful email, expressing my discomfort with her presence and general existence, reiterating that I had wanted to invite only family. Then at the end of the letter, I asked him outright not to bring her.

In a move that defecated on my feelings, my father, in so many words, reminded me that he was the father and I was his daughter. He wouldn't take orders from me, and if she couldn't come, then, well, he was sorry, but neither could he.

My nose crinkled with the tears that I refused to shed. I was shocked—and further convinced that this woman had him under an evil, rancid vaginal spell. My mother was livid and so were his sisters, who scolded him for his misguided allegiance. By the time of the show, my family arrived to support me, without him. The morning of the show, Lamine handed me an envelope from my dad. Inside, there was a check for five hundred dollars with a note that read, "Good luck. Love, Dad." I asked my brother to return it to him, which I honestly went back and forth about because Lord knows I was a broke-ass college student.

He did eventually come up a month later for my graduation, without her. With my older brothers, my mother's sister, and my grandparents present, I'd like to think he put more thought into it.

As the years followed, and I found myself in New York and then back in Los Angeles under my mother's roof, I started to visit my father more frequently, especially since a few things had evolved. One, he had moved into a house in Ladera Heights, and while his new whore would stay over occasionally, she still kept her mansion in the marina to herself. Also, my brother's studio was in my father's house, and he would find me there every Sunday, shooting episodes of my second web series, *Fly Guys present "The 'F' Word,"* a comedic mockumentary starring my brother and his rap group's attempts to "make it" in Los Angeles. Despite my father's complaints about the occasional noise, I could tell he enjoyed having us in his house, particularly when Lamine, Elize, and I would be there together. By that time, the three of us were well aware of the extent of the "cultural differences" that had transpired between our parents. Lastly, in 2009, the summer I moved to L.A., my sister and I took another trip to Senegal to see my family and to have some Sene-fun. During that trip, I realized it's nearly impossible to be in my father's home country, amongst his family, and not be appreciative of his existence. The respect people there have for him and for all that he's done for them is overwhelming. Repeated proclamations of "Your father is such a great man," and the excitement with which "Oh, you are the kids of Dr. Diop!" was uttered, restored some of the pride I had in my father as a man. Finally, I had to come to terms with the fact that my father is not a bad person. He's just . . . a flawed man.

As the schedule for shooting *Fly Guys* became more consistent, and my dad started to grow more accustomed to seeing me on the weekends (and often during the week), he started to bring food home for me, sometimes calling in advance to ensure I was there or leaving it in the fridge for me to come claim. As broke as I was during those times, it was always appreciated. On one of the evenings, our schedules aligned serendipitously and we were able to eat together. I sat and ate at the kitchen bar, discussing international news with him while he watched MSNBC on the couch, when suddenly I had a bout of déjà vu. Nothing dramatic, just a tingle and mild dizziness that reminded me I had been in that particular situation before. My déjà vu is pretty useless. It doesn't provide any insight other than, "Oh hey, you went through this at some point in the universe's spectrum of time. Don't know when, or how, or what this means, but just thought you should know."

I came back from my two-second zone-out and casually muttered, "Déjà vu," and that's when my dad nonchalantly decided to expose me to my potential powers.

"Oh, you know that runs in our family."

"What?"

"Déjà vu. It's our family gift. Your grandmother had it. Her grandmother has it. Some of your aunts have it. I had it, but I didn't want it."

He took a bite out of his sandwich, the Brie and cranberry dripping out onto his plate. I looked at him with the skepticism I always did when he joked about abnormal things.

"You're joking, right?"

"No. Ask your aunts. You could have it, too, if you want to."

"How did you know you had it? What does it do?"

"I just knew. One day, when I was in school, my friend and I were walking at night, down a steep hill. There was an alley at the bottom of the hill which ends at the corner. I had déjà vu and my friend asked, 'What's wrong with you?' and I said someone is going to come around that corner from the alley on their moped and they're going to fall. My friend laughed and said, 'You're crazy!' A minute later, someone came on a moped, turned the corner fast, and fell. My friend put his hand on his head and said, 'Oh my God!' "

My dad laughed at the memory of his bewildered friend as I sat frozen, forehead bewildered.

"So . . . you don't have it anymore?" I asked.

"No, I didn't want it. Some people know what to do with it. I didn't want to think about it."

I thought about the famous line from *Spider-Man* when Uncle Ben tells Peter Parker, right before Peter indirectly causes his death, "With great power comes great responsibility." My dad didn't want to be held responsible. Little did he know back then that he would be held responsible (financially) for many of my family members in the future. For the sake of his bank account, he should have tapped into his déjà vu to see that shit. Or at least turn it on and off to see which decisions were worth making and which weren't. Who knows what direction life would have taken him.

Recently, my dad has been trying to spend time with my younger sister and brother and me in the form of monthly lunches. He will usually send us an obscure text that says "sushi???" or "Korean BBQ???" out of the blue, and my sister Elize and I will coordinate to include my brother Lamine, who is often forgotten because he works at my dad's office every day and thus sees him all the time. These family lunches are a highlight for me. Not only because of the laughter and inside jokes my siblings and I share, but also because they are an opportunity to get inside my father's mind. We learn something new at each session. Without our prying too deeply, he'll occasionally volunteer information to us.

"I'm going to sell the property I have in Dakar," he said at one lunch, as he flipped a thin slab of raw beef onto the hot grill in front of us.

Many times, the information that he offers reached us long ago, through my mother or other family members. But to hear it from him directly is always to hear a more toned-down, "it is what it is" version.

One winter day, we were sitting at lunch—me, Elize, and my father—eating at Hillstone (even though it was his idea to go to a steakhouse, he ordered the trout). I had the book on my mind and decided to fact-check.

"Dad, did you and mom meet in Bordeaux, France, or in Senegal, first?"

My sister jumped in, like we were playing Family Trivial Pursuit. "France, right? Even I know that."

"Yes, it was Bordeaux," my dad answered, taking another bite of trout.

"Okay, and then she went to Senegal?" I confirmed.

"Yes, she didn't go to Senegal until later," he said with a nod.

Then he stopped cutting, and acknowledged something that had been bothering me for the twelve years since they broke up.

"I guess we never really had a conversation about what happened, did we?"

I froze. *UH, F\*\*\*ING DUH!!!* Rapid-fire flashbacks of tears, unanswered questions, missed college performances, and pensive diary entries raced through my head. Was he really about to use his *words* and not only acknowledge the divorce, but *talk to us* about what happened?

Just weeks earlier, I'd had brunch with Andunett, one of my childhood fellow nomad friends—actually, my only nomad friend. It had been several years since we'd sat down and caught each other up on our respective lives. She was briefly in town from Tennessee, venting that she wanted to return to Los Angeles, but the thought of living with her mom again was enough to keep her hungry and uncomfortable in Tennessee. Her mom is Ethiopian but actually grew up in Senegal with my aunts. We laughed about trying to have honest conversations with our respective African parents about our feelings. In a brief moment of sincerity, I revealed to her that I wish I could get inside my father's head, that I could talk to him about the divorce, about his choice in women, just to get a sense of where his head was. But I shrugged, noting that my Senegalese father would never be open to such candid conversation and prodding questions from his daughter. Andunett nodded with understanding.

Now, as I sat before my dad, my heartbeat revealed the surprise that my face tried to hide as I feigned nonchalance and tried to keep my tone casually delicate, so as not to lose the rare opportunity for a truth viewing.

"So," I started. "What happened?"

My dad explained, between long gazes at his food and our respective faces, that after Elize was born, during our last year in Senegal, he wanted to go back to Los Angeles, but my mother had no interest in returning there. They both agreed that he would try to make it work in Los Angeles and she would take us to Maryland.

"But whenever I would visit you all in Potomac, I felt out of place. Your mother had an established way of doing things and I started feeling a sense of detachment."

By the time we had arrived in Los Angeles to reunite with him, he explained, he didn't know us as well as our mom did, and whenever he would try to intervene in certain aspects of raising us, our mother would have already established the right way to do it—and that the distance definitely played a huge part in their unraveling. As he explained, he made no excuses, didn't fault our mother or ever speak ill of her. Hearing him talk about it and acknowledge what happened gave me a sense of closure and comfort in knowing that I could actually talk to him about it. About anything, really.

———

My father is now remarried, settling in with his new wife. And though I find myself tip-toeing around her with forced politeness, I don't find myself as hesitant to get inside his head. When I'm ready to go down that road, I will.

Today, with the Obamacare California deadline looming, my dad calls me to make sure I have health insurance.

"Hey, Dad," I answer.

"Sign up for the California Care. Google it and tell your sister."

I'm driving on Edgewood to a meeting in Hollywood.

"Dad, I *been* had insurance. I'm grown," I say playfully, laughing because my dad still doesn't know exactly what it is that I do. He's just grateful I'm not on his payroll anymore. He laughs heartily. "Oh, you're grown? How many bills am I paying again?"

*Oops.* "Oh, just kidding. I was just playing. I'm not grown,

Dad!" I relent as I realize he's still paying my phone bill (I'm on a family plan). And my car insurance (that shit's expensive). And up until that conversation, which must have served as a reminder for him, my car was still in his name. No less than a week later, he gave me the pink slip of ownership. Now all my tickets go directly to *me*.

I realize I can get so caught up in my own feelings that I forget how much my dad still does for me, without a single complaint. I neglect to consider how much he will continue to support me, no matter what I need, as long as he can. While I still haven't heard the words "I love you," I realize I haven't said them to him either. We both have some feelings to catch up on and I know I'm not beyond initiating them.

# Dating Lessons & Summer Lust

The Diop women—including those who marry into the family—haven't had a great history with men. I observed this only in the last few years, when one of my favorite Senegalese aunts, whose chill demeanor and laid-back beauty I've always admired, married a man who was absolutely hideous in every way. His face looked like God said, "I just . . . I can't. I'm tired. Let me see what I can do with these leftovers." I don't ever call people ugly and if his personality didn't match his appearance, then his looks wouldn't be an issue. But after meeting him, it was abundantly clear that she was settling for some kind of security. This was the aunt I was proud to say my high school boyfriend had a crush on. She was the aunt who I hoped to look and be like when I grew up.

Twelve years prior, my aunt married a handsome Senegalese man who lived in the house across the street from our family home. We met him during one of our yearly visits, and he seemed to be well favored among the aunties. My aunt gave birth to her first child while she was staying with us in Los Angeles. She was the most adorable little girl ever, and the first child whose birth I remember, whose diaper (singular, because it happened only once) I remember changing, and who I happily cradled and put to sleep on several occasions. She was the daughter my aunt always wanted.

Soon after the birth, my aunt's marriage ended. Long-distance relationships are already hard to make work, so a cross-continental relationship was bound for failure. At the time, I attributed the end of their marriage to that alone.

Then I grew up, took a step back, and took stock of my dad and his six siblings. We already know my father's marital situation (more on that in "African Dad"), and the other situationships on his side of the family didn't fare much better. Out of his four sisters, none of the marriages lasted, for reasons that varied, from polygamy[5] to adultery to fatal freak accident. Where the Diop men are concerned (i.e., my dad's brothers), the curse is transmitted by name to the women they marry. There may be a loophole in marrying a Diop and not taking on the last name, but I have been unable to find evidence in that just yet. No marriage is without its problems, but I think I can trace the curse back to my grandfather, who, with his infidelities, also extended our family beyond that which he created with my grandmother. Perhaps that's where the curse began? The Senegalese are no stranger to curses, spells, and jinxes. Perhaps, in being unfaithful to my loyal grandmother, my grandfather unknowingly solidified the fate of his children to a life of cursed romances and marriages. Or maybe the French culture's casual embrace of flings coupled with Islam's encouragement of "responsible polygamy" plays into our "curse." Maybe it's not that

---

5  Polygamy is legal in Senegal, which is a predominantly Muslim country.

big of a deal, as one of my father's Senegalese friends once told my mother, "It's our God-given right to have a mistress." *Oh. Well, then.*

Between my family history, its cultural and religious affinity for infidelity, and the American divorce statistics, I've held firm to the belief that if I don't get married, that would be just fine. Marriage will never be a priority for me. Even now, as I hear about relationships ending around me and marriages "failing" (as opposed to "passing," I suppose), and people deceiving one another, sometimes losing tons of money in the process, I think, *What's the point of getting married?* For one thing, marriage seems to have become a bit of a national joke. There are reality shows for gold-diggers while televised Bridezillas and messy infidelities get sky-high ratings. To think that amidst all the infidelity, Americans actually had the nerve to try to get all sanctimonious when the gay marriage debate surfaced. Shut up!

My indifference to marriage doesn't mean I won't commit to someone. I'm in a relationship as I write this, one to which I've been committed for over seven years, though the path here has been anything but easy.

Trouble started as early as high school, where people thought I was a lesbian because of the way I dressed. It didn't help that I didn't know that rainbows were an LGBT symbol and would frequently color all of my name tags with the colors of the rainbow.

In college, things started to get a bit better. In time a few guys asked me out, but negatively influenced by my parents' divorce, I went through a chronic cheating phase. For one thing, I didn't want to feel too attached to any one person, after witnessing my mother's feelings of betrayal and violation in light of my father's affair. In my mind, it was cheat or be cheated on, and I felt a sense of satisfaction knowing that I had beat my partner to the punch—whether he knew it or not. This way, if he decided to cheat, then I would be numb to it because I had done it first. It's a really juvenile way of thinking, an emotional escape route that would allow me to leave with just the clothes on my back when necessary.

By my junior year of college, my prospects, if not my attitude, had started to improve. I came back to college a little bit thinner and with a perfectly white, straight smile, thanks to five years of braces. I noticed the change almost immediately. I started getting more attention from guys and started to seek it in a completely different way than I did during my desperate middle and high school years. I wasn't interested in a relationship; I just wanted sexual activity. Because I had stopped out of school the year prior, I missed out on the housing draw, and I learned over the summer that I would be in a one-room double with a stranger in the quiet study dorm. NOPE. Wasn't having that. So I told my dad that I wanted to live off-campus, somehow convincing him that it would be significantly cheaper because he wouldn't have to pay for a meal plan, my two jobs would allow me to buy groceries, and I would be able to help him with the rent (I didn't, and he wouldn't have allowed it anyway). I found an apartment that was a five-minute drive from campus and moved in early, elated. I felt an overwhelming sense of liberation as I held the keys in my hand. I didn't have any furniture to my name and I didn't care. After a night on the carpeted floor, I woke up the next morning and headed to IKEA, equipped with my very first credit card—a Discover card with a limit of one thousand dollars, the most I'd ever had in my account at one time.

With my new apartment, my own car, and my very own credit card, I developed a new independence. I could do whatever I wanted. Barring my being enrolled in college, I was a grown-ass woman and I could do grown-ass woman things in the privacy of my grown-ass woman home. The two years I spent in that apartment were two of the best years of my life—in terms of my friendships, my creativity, my relationships, and my sense of identity.

The first boyfriend to set foot in my man-eating apartment was George. We met while I was home during a weekend in Los Angeles. He was super attractive, with a smile with which I fell in lust. We went on a date to the movies and our chemistry was palpable. He was genuinely sweet and adorably shy and spoke with one of those hybrid London-Nigerian accents. When I drove back up to Stanford, we talked every single day. He was going to school to study business and was intent on returning to Nigeria to become the president someday. I was impressed with his ambition. Then one day, he called me with embarrassment and anger.

"I got kicked out of school."

"*What?* What happened?"

"I kicked this guy's ass for talking shit."

I was silent on the other end. I had never been with a guy who had kicked anyone's ass before. While I was disappointed that he was expelled, the simple bitch in me was impressed.

"Hello?" he asked.

"You kicked a guy's—what happened?"

"He was just all in my face, talking shit and asking for it. I lost my temper and now I have to figure out what to do."

I wasn't terribly worried about him. There were countless schools in Los Angeles, and surely he could enroll in a community college while he applied to a new school. Only a couple of days later, he called me with some more news.

"I'm going to be a Marine."

"Like a swimmer?"

"No, like the military. The Marine Corps."

We had known each other only a month, but he'd managed to leave me speechless twice in one week.

"Why," I asked. "Do you have a death wish?" We were still in a war and, in my mind, he would certainly be deployed to go fight. I had been reading every day about suicide bombings and mass military rapes and women and children being killed mercilessly. Why would anyone who had options want to voluntarily subject himself to that? I didn't see bravery; I saw stupidity. But George was determined. He wasn't asking my permission; he was just gauging how I felt about his decision. I hated it, but it didn't matter.

"Well, I saw a recruiter today and if I'm accepted, I go to boot camp in three weeks." *Why did he even call me?!*

"But the good news," he continued, "is that I can come spend the weekend with you before I go." My mind and loins raced. He would be the first gentleman visitor in my new place. I tried to play it cool, while still being outraged that he would decide to embark upon this suicide mission without actually taking my feelings into consideration.

"Well, you'd better."

He made plans to come up by Greyhound bus a few weeks later. Most of my friends had taken trips abroad, and so I had no one to call and get advice from except Suzanne, one of my high school best friends who attended UC Berkeley. She wasn't that experienced with gentleman callers, so couldn't offer any advice beyond "Have fun!"

I picked him up from the bus station bumping Rasheeda's provocative "Georgia Peach," just in case he needed some subliminal signals as to what was about to go down. In case that wasn't enough, I had lit "smell-good" candles all around my house to set the mood. I had fleeting thoughts of returning home only to find my apartment engulfed in flames, with Gemma my Fargo-accented landlord "Gee golly"-ing in horror. But when I pulled up to find him waiting at that bus stop, a single duffel bag in hand, smiling with contained excitement to see me, I didn't give a damn about any fires.

I watched him walk to my window. He leaned his head in and smiled.

"You're not gonna get out and give me a hug?"

I promptly swung my door open and hopped into his arms. Then we shared our very first kiss.

When we got back in the car, I popped in a 50 Cent CD, his favorite rapper of all time, and we headed back to my place.

George was my first relationship since my high school boyfriend, and now he was leaving me to go become a soldier. I'm pretty positive I cried after he left. We'd known each other for only a couple of months, and while his incessant back-to-back phone calls and "hey" texts would annoy me, I still missed him. A topic we frequently broached, and that George was often too eager to talk about, was Laila, his ex-girlfriend who still lived in London. I'm not the jealous type, but I'm the jealous type. Appearance-wise, I didn't feel threatened. Feelings-wise, I did. Laila was George's first love and she dumped him. I'm always wary about guys who've been dumped by girls they loved, because it typically means they have unresolved feelings. George didn't hide the fact that he'd enjoyed the years they spent together, but he frequently insisted that he was completely over her. This didn't stop him from putting her in his Top 8 on his MySpace page, however. The Top 8 was like a public acknowledgment of one's clique, a blanket endorsement of the people with whom one associates heavily. Because she lived in London, however, I was willing to excuse this as a simple oversight on his part.

When George graduated from boot camp, I was there. I made

the trip to the San Diego base, excited to be reunited with him, fantasizing that he'd pick me up and carry me across the auditorium, as Richard Gere did to Debra Winger in *An Officer and a Gentleman.* I think I was oblivious to the fact that my friends' absence had caused me to gain weight—having no one to hang with left lots of time for quality snack time. So when we were finally reunited, George's first words to me were, "Damn, girl, you've been eating good." I think I can safely pinpoint that as the moment at which my insecurity about our relationship started.

This was also the first time I met George's mother, his sisters, and his brother. They were all nice enough, but I felt inadequate— partly because Laila had made such a positive impression on his family before I was in the picture, and mostly because I hadn't been faithful during George's thirteen-week stint in boot camp. Over the course of his absence, we exchanged letters, but I found that just wasn't enough for me. Plus, his enthusiasm to be a Marine and shoot guns and kill people wasn't exactly compatible with my liberal, nonviolent views. So, when opportunity knocked, I answered, justifying my infidelity by telling myself that he still had feelings for his ex-girlfriend anyway. Still, a part of me felt guilty. Until, that is, I returned home from his graduation, where I was only able to spend a brief couple of hours with him as he stayed behind with his family, who had come all the way from London. Back home, I logged on to MySpace a few days later. It was during a bout of bored curiosity—which is typically the mood in which if you seek, you shall find—that I clicked on his ex's page, and there for all the world to see was a heartfelt wall message from George, addressing her as "baby." I was angry, slightly hurt, but mostly livid about what I perceived to be public disrespect. Nobody really knew about our relationship, but how dare he?

I called him and immediately ended our relationship. Over the next couple of weeks, he called me back to back, apologizing, begging for my forgiveness. I grew satisfied as my hurt feelings turned to general irritation. Plus, by that time, I had already moved on with Taz.

Taz, ruggedly handsome and with brash confidence, would probably drive a girl with low self-esteem to suicide. Had I met him during my high school years, I would have either succumbed to his blunt aggression or tucked myself away, deciding that I was out of his league. However, he met me during a time when I felt my confidence rising. I'd started to feel more comfortable in my skin, as many college students tend to; never mind that I knew absolutely *nothing* about life. I was amused by Taz's hot temper, which was cutely mismatched with a deep, raspy French accent. When he grew upset with a joke I made at his expense, he sounded like a peeved Pepé Le Pew.

Taz was generally extremely closed off, more so than I was, which drew me to him. An heir to his father's prosperous textile business, he attended school in Pittsburgh and held a 4.0 GPA, despite English being his second language. Even with his academic obligations, he managed to talk to me on the phone at three in the morning Eastern time every other night. With each conversation, he'd let me in more and more, and we grew to appreciate each other's opposite senses of humor.

Taz and I had a strong sexual attraction to each other, one I still can't explain. But to that end, our relationship was often volatile. He could make me irate in a way that I didn't know I could be and vice versa. Though we were never officially an item, he was insanely jealous of my time, and I, too, wasn't unaffected by his love for women. When we were great, we were amazing. When we weren't, it was severe. All these factors, despite his dedication to seeing me as often as he could, made me decide internally never to pursue a serious relationship with him. Though we remained in touch throughout the school year, we would each pursue other love interests, much to his dismay.

By the time summer rolled around, I decided not to go home to Los Angeles. I had an apartment and freedom, so why would I? I took a temporary volunteer gig in Menlo Park as an after-school workshop instructor in the arts for kids aged twelve to seventeen. The only thing I remember about those kids was that not *one* of them knew who Michael Jackson was, which made me wonder what kind of sad kids Menlo Park was raising.

I met Oladife at the grocery store during the summer where my best girlfriends, Megan and Akilah, and I took a vow to be open-minded to everything that came our way. We made this decision specifically to add peer pressure to the youngest member of our trio, Akilah, whose standards for men were ridiculously high, undoubtedly based on her virginal status. So we made a pact to resist the inclination to say "no." Every time one of us would consider backing out, we'd simultaneously guilt trip one another by trailing off the refrain, "I mean we *did* say . . ."

So that summer afternoon, when he approached me in the aisle of Safeway, nearly two inches shorter than me, with a colonial English and South African hybrid accent, I shrugged and said, "I mean we *did* say . . ."

But Oladife was just too much. He wanted to be romantic far too quickly (and not even in the sexual sense, which would have made me have a bit more respect for him, but in an emotional way that absolutely grossed me out). After going out on one date with him, I realized that he took himself and his feelings far too seriously;

this was evidenced by the verses of poetry he texted me the same day we met. *Ew*.

I don't even remember what we did on our first date, honestly. My memory is quick to efface and shield me from the irrelevant. Before I'm subject to harsh judgment, I'd like to assert that my callousness can't be attributed to "nice guy" unappreciation. He wasn't a nice guy in the sweet, gentlemanly sense; he was overbearing in his attempts to suck me into his fog of emotions. I've dated and politely turned down nice guys before and felt super bad about it; this was not one of those times.

I do remember that we hung out close to Stanford's campus and at the end of the night, we found ourselves near the posh plaza adjacent to Embarcadero Road, one of Palo Alto's main streets. I recall this part of the date only because it was then that he kept trying to hold my hand. Listen, I'll let you stick your tongue in my mouth before I let you hold my hand. It's mostly because of my own insecurities. The condensation that can brew between the heated concave part of hands that touch is enough to drive me insane. Also, I have big hands with long, skinny fingers, and whenever I have to hold hands with people (in prayer or to help them safely cross the street), I'm worried that they will a) comment on the size of my hands, à la "Damn! You got some big-ass hands for a woman!" or b) remark how disgustingly sweaty my palms are as they pull theirs away. Or worse, not say anything at all and just endure my sweaty hands hoping I don't notice them abruptly wipe their own hands immediately after we disengage. But in this particular instance, because my empathy gland is oversized and it pains me to be the cause of hurt feelings and rejection, I briefly obliged his third attempt to lock my hand to his. If only I had the visual defense mechanism that porcupines do. If only my hands were equipped with quills to defend me from the fingertip rubs he inflicted on the lines of my palms. *Are you trying to predict my future mid-stroll, mother$#@%?&!* I thought, furious with myself for my genetic failings.

I couldn't take it anymore. I made up a reason I needed to go home and, fortunately, he obliged and drove me back to my apartment. No later than two minutes after I had barricaded my door behind me, heaving with the relief of freedom, I received a phone call. Worried that he would come back if I didn't answer, I picked up.

"Hello?"

"Look at the moon."

I paused. "What?"

"Look at the mooooon," he whispered tenderly.

"What about it?" I asked, tapping my fingers with impatience.

"Are you looking at it?" he prodded.

"I am." I was not.

"I'm looking at it, too . . . I just wanted you to know that. So you'll think of me and know that I'm thinking of you whenever you look at the night sky."

I felt my vagina dry and shrivel up, like a raisin in the sun.

"Unh-huh," I managed, incredulous.

"Good night," he cooed, then he slowly and softly traced every button on his phone before he hung up. Probably.

After days of curt responses to his texts and avoiding his phone calls, I wrote him a carefully crafted text, telling him I wasn't looking for a serious relationship. He called me and told me it was my loss. Oladife made me realize how much I hate overly sentimental gestures—especially if they're from the wrong guy.

The final month of summer, my friends and I got into work mode, making sure we'd be set up financially for the impending school year. Megan was working at a law firm, making connections to secure an opportunity the following year. Akilah, who worked at a tutoring program, was helping middle school kids get ready for their upcoming school year. I had gotten another job—my dream job, a position I've wanted since I was nine years old. Ever since my little brother, Lamine, and I simulated owning a fast-food restaurant called Hamburgers Everywhere! I've had ambitions of owning a restaurant or being a waitress. Nine-year-old me clearly thought the two were interchangeable. When I got a job as a waitress at the new Counter burger restaurant in Palo Alto, I got to see a restaurant built and managed from the ground up and learned that my stress levels would be more fit for waitressing. Aside from some shitty managers and a couple of horrible co-workers, I loved waitressing. Even today, I maintain that if nothing works out in my life, I would be content working as a waitress.

I met Martin while serving tables during one of our busy lunch shifts. He wasn't in my section, but I kept passing by his table, making sure he had everything he needed. He smiled politely and shook his head. After the third attempt with no words exchanged between us, I shrugged. Well, I tried. And just as he was getting up to leave, he spoke. In a heavy French accent, he asked me my name.

"*Tu parles Français?*" I tried.

He told me he was from France by way of Martinique and was in the country for a stage, or a paid internship, working for a food service/supply company. Yup, he could get it. We exchanged numbers and I marveled at my luck. What were the odds of my meeting another cute French guy? At the very least, I'd have a new opportunity to practice the language.

Martin and I kept it casual, going on a couple of dates here and there. I was still talking to Taz, from Pittsburgh by way of France, every night, when he decided to make another trip to see me in Palo

Alto. By this time, we had switched to our third manager at The Counter, a man who started off nice enough but then transformed into a merciless tyrant, in an attempt to assert his power. Taz's visit meant I had to ask for time off during the weekend, our busiest time. Because I knew the manager would never approve of me taking days off because "a friend was in town," I decided to lie about my circumstances. In a prophetic lie I'd come to regret for the rest of my life, I told him I had to go help my aunt in Oakland, who was sick. In any case, it worked, and Taz and I spent the entire weekend together, acting like a couple and . . . fighting like one. While we had a great, fiery chemistry, that weekend only solidified for me that I could not be in a relationship with him. Consequently, I never allowed my feelings for Taz to develop simply because when I pictured our future, I saw a vulnerable me. Call me a coward, but that just wouldn't do. Taz made me realize what I *don't* want in a relationship. I don't ever want to be at the mercy of my emotions—that's fun and adventurous for some people, but not me.

When Martin asked me to be his girlfriend, I accepted. Taz flipped out when I told him, frustrated that I wouldn't give us a chance. I told him I didn't trust him enough to be in a committed relationship with him, and he stopped talking to me for over six months. In the meantime, I got to know Martin more. We spoke only in French, and he was one of the most affectionate guys I'd ever been with, which he could sense. Prior to making our relationship official, we were friends with benefits. Or so I thought.

One night he called me to ask if he could come over and hang out. I told him I was on my period. He got silent and asked, "What does that have to do with anything?" Embarrassed, I said, "Oh, I just thought you should know. But come anyway." When he came, we sat on my bed watching movies and he asked me again, "Why did you tell me you were on your period?" Truthfully, it was be-cause I expected our "quality time" to be centered only around sex. I told him otherwise.

"Just in case I was moody, I didn't want you to be offended."

He nodded, and I thought he bought it, but he didn't. One day, a couple of weeks later, he asked me if he could come over and talk. I had no idea what he wanted to talk to me about. That evening, he walked in the door, looking more somber than I had ever seen him.

"I don't think you like me very much," he started.

"What? What are you talking about?" I asked.

"Oftentimes, I will call you and you won't call me back. Or when I come over to spend time with you, you'll just go to sleep. And then that period thing. What are we doing?"

As I listened to him go on about what he wasn't getting from me in our "relationship," I grew confused—what was this?

I opted for the truth. "Honestly, I thought we were just . . ." *Shit*—what were the French words for "friends with benefits"?

"What did you think we were 'just'?" he insisted.

I scrambled to put words together without sounding vulgar. It was the first language-barrier issue we'd encountered. I kept repeat-ing the words in English, hoping he'd understand what "benefits" meant, but the more and more I said it, the dumber I felt. Frustrated, he proposed a solution. "I think we should stop seeing each other, since you don't like me."

I was shocked. I had never been broken up with before, much less from someone with whom I didn't even know I was in a rela-tionship. But if this was what he wanted, then who was I to stop him? Not his girlfriend, apparently. I nodded. "If that's what you think is best." As I walked him to the door, I found myself starting to get emotional. It had been two months of seeing each other, after all, and the thought of not seeing him or spending any time with him actually made me sad. As I opened the door for him, he turned around to hug me but stopped when he saw tears in my eyes.

"Are you actually sad?"

"I don't know. Maybe."

This sign of emotion was apparently enough for him to reconsider his decision. He kissed me, picked me up off the floor like I weighed thirty pounds, and we made up. An hour later, Martin asked me one more time to explain what a "friend with benefits" was. When I did, he told me, "We don't do that in France." Then he asked me to be his girlfriend.

As our relationship progressed and Martin and I started practically living together, he introduced the topic of meeting my friends.

"Why haven't you introduced me to your friends? Are you ashamed of me?"

I laughed. "Of course not. I hadn't really thought about it."

But the truth was, I had. My friends were pressing me about meeting him, calling him my "secret lover." The problem was, Martin had this cornrow/braid combo situation going on that I hated. It was 2006, and men with braids after the age of twenty-one were either thugs or painfully out of touch. I didn't want to tell him to cut it, because I didn't want to hurt his feelings. I didn't want to appear shallow, but I had never introduced a boyfriend to my college friends before and I wanted the presentation to be perfect.

The day he casually mentioned that he felt like cutting all his hair off, my enthusiasm was on eleven. "Yes! Absolutely! Try something new! Go for it!"

As soon as he unveiled his new look, a freshly cut fade with a neatly trimmed five-o'clock shadow, I was in love. Was I that superficial? I guess. His haircut timing happened to coincide with a Winter Comedy event, thrown by Megan's sorority, Alpha Kappa Alpha. This would be the perfect opportunity to unveil him to my friends. I invited him out, waiting a few days so as not to seem obvious about my sudden interest in showing him off.

"Hey, do you want to go to this comedy show? You can meet my friends."

He smiled, seeing right through me. "So, it was the hair."

The comedy show was a great time, and my friends approved of him. I was so relieved to have that out of the way.

Martin and I were getting closer, but his internship deadline, which had already been extended, was rapidly approaching. This meant he'd be going back to France, relegating our closeness to long distance. While my feelings for him were strong, this fact was hovering over my heart and my head. I started wondering if I was really ready to try to make it work with him while he was so far away. I was only twenty-one, and after many awkward years, I was just starting to enjoy guys being into me.

Plus, Martin had a trait that drove me nuts: he loved to argue, in an often condescending manner. At twenty-five, he was four years older than me, though he acted as if it were more like ten. Like many people, I don't like being told what to do, nor do I like to be made to feel inferior under any circumstances.

In one particular incident, I had just started to gear up for "Stan-Funk," a show put on during homecoming weekend for alumni and undergraduates alike. I had been asked to direct the show and was honored to be a part of it. Martin had decided to drop me off at rehearsals that night, as he was planning on spending the night. We were early, so we parked in front of the rehearsal space. I had to get some paperwork ready and started filling it out in the car, but the pen I was using had no ink, so I threw it out the window. Martin turned to me from the driver's seat.

"Go pick that up."

Maybe it was his tone, or his stern look, or the imperative "*va*" in French that triggered my anger, but I snapped. My anger at all the times he'd talked down to me had accumulated and it burst forth at once. He was going to hear all of my grievances in his car that night, very loudly.

His eyes widened in surprise when I started, and when I was done, he sat silently, looking ahead. As I calmed down, my anger slowly subsiding, I started to think about his command and my response. Had he simply said, "Come on, don't do that" in a tone that appealed to my typical environmental sensitivity, things would have been fine. But there was an edge to his demand and the way he condescended to me that I knew I could never tolerate. Despite that, I regretted my temper and my harsh words, and when I got out of the car to go to rehearsal, I picked up the pen. When I handed him the pen through his open window, he turned his face to me and said, "I would have had more respect for you if you'd just left it there." *Really, asshole?*

While his words gut-punched my ego, I retorted, "I didn't do it for you." Still, my relationship escape route was clearly etched in my mind from that day forward. I had one for every relationship, influenced negatively by my parents' divorce. So when my cousin Aida called me one day, out of the blue, and asked if she could give her friend Louis my number, I found myself open.

"He saw your pictures and he keeps asking me about you," she said, with a hint of irritation.

"Really?" I was surprised. Louis was gorgeous: tall, with the athletic build of a football player and Blasian features, on account of his Senegalese and Vietnamese background. During the summer, I had seen his picture on Hi5, an international MySpace I used from time to time to keep up with my cousins and friends, before they caught on to Facebook. My cousin Amadou, Aida's brother, was also friends with him, and so I added him, thinking nothing of it. I was pleasantly surprised, then, when Louis sent me a message: "hi there . . ." We engaged in a few two-sentence messages back and forth, but he never really asked me about myself, and so the conversation quickly died. Now, nearly four months later, he had emerged and asked for my number through my younger cousin. *Why didn't he just ask me?* I shrugged. Whatever, he was fine.

Martin and I were walking around a Safeway grocery store, shopping for dinner, when Louis first called me. I ignored the call because I didn't recognize the number. When I listened to his voicemail, my stomach churned with butterflies of excitement. I told Martin I was going to go look for some vegetables in another aisle and escaped to listen to the message again. I called Louis back and got his voice mail. I quickly left a message, saying I was happy he'd called and that I'd try him back another time. I skipped over to Martin in the pasta aisle and we resumed shopping.

The night I drove home for Christmas break, I called Louis . . . from a blocked number. He answered but I hung up. What the hell was wrong with me? I couldn't ignore the memories of my previous dating disappointments. He had seen my pictures, he had already asked for my number; why was this an issue? I practiced my "sexy phone voice" and then dialed, with my number visible. He answered.

"Hello?"

"Hi," I started with a tone that screamed phone sex operator.

I shook my head and cleared my throat. I didn't have to do this. I could be myself. I continued in my normal voice.

"Sorry, allergies. Hi, it's great to finally talk to you."

As corny as it sounds, from the very first five-hour conversation Louis and I had, I knew he was the one for me; that he would be the one I'd end up with, the one I wanted.

The night before Martin went back to France, we had the worst sex ever. It was so selfish that I'm still bitter about it to this day. Maybe I deserved it. No matter what, I knew that despite the promises we'd made to try to make it work long distance, our relationship was officially over.

I don't know whether or not Louis and I will be together forever, but I know that I genuinely love him and that he has made me a better person, which is more than I've gotten out of any other relationship.

With him, I've finally come to the conclusion that my parents' relationship doesn't have to inform my own. I've taken off the safety.

# ABG Guide:
# Black Women & Asian Men

Black women and Asian men are at the bottom of the dating totem pole in the United States. Yes, it's true. After many discussions and several observations over the years, I've decided that this is the case, and said as much as early as 2010.

If dating were an assortment of Halloween candy, black women and Asian men would be the Tootsie Rolls and candy corn—the last to be eaten, if even at all (if you like Tootsie Rolls and candy corn, it is a FACT that you have dated/would date an Asian man/black woman[6]). Why is this? Why will over 45 percent of educated black women never get married? Why are Asian men so high in supply but so low in demand? I can offer a few explanations and guesses, based on snippets of conversation, credible news outlets, and Steve Harvey.

---

6 Not based on fact.

Educated black women are too high maintenance, high strung, and independent—they don't need men. There is a widening gap between the education of black women and men, which doesn't leave very many "suitable" suitors. Unfortunately, the higher one's degree, as a black woman, the lower your chances are of getting married. Add to the con pile the stereotypes of being loud, complicated, and difficult. Black women, your reputation sucks.

Asian men are also overburdened with racial stereotypes that don't really work in their favor. Why wouldn't women want to marry and reproduce with men who are classified as intelligent hard workers? Maybe because Asian men are frequently emasculated in the media, or presented as sexless props, for comedic relief. Oh, if only they could absorb the burden of black male stereotypes (genitalia exaggerations included), maybe their demand would increase. Maybe that would make all the difference. Instead, the plight of Asian men is nearly the same as that of black women, except for the fact that their women tend to marry white or "other" far more often. In fact, Asian Americans have the highest rate of intermarriage. Asian men, your reputation sucks too.

This is why I propose that black women and Asian men join forces in love, marriage, and procreation. Educated black women, what better intellectual match for you than an Asian man? And I'm not talking about Filipinos; they're like the blacks of Asians. I'm talking Chinese, Vietnamese, Japanese, et cetera. According to a 2010 census, Koreans are more inclined to marry black than any other Asian group. So black women, after college, maybe it's a good idea to settle in Los Angeles or anywhere else where Koreatown is a hotspot. Asian men, your women are ditching you at an alarming rate; won't you consider black women? Especially YOU, Chinese men—there is an abundance of you, and you're not all going to get Chinese women . . . so why not cross over to the black side? Have you all seen how adorable Blasian babies are? Get with the program.

# Musical Ambitions & Failures

The smell of Black & Milds evokes a nostalgia for the hoodrat childhood of which I was robbed. If a CD had a "Parental Advisory: Explicit Content" label, I was forbidden from enjoying it, which meant I was excluded from the vending machine conversations in middle school. While my thirteen-year-old girlfriends whispered about Lil Kim's racy *Hardcore* album and the No Limit Soldiers' music takeover, I was relegated to the role of "silent listener." On a rare occasion, I could at least contribute to conversations about music videos, except for those found only on that pay-per-video channel, The Box. Those too eluded me as, you guessed it, the cable at my house didn't carry The Box, so I had to catch it at my grandparents' house.

My affinity for my generation's music almost never was. While I have always been an R&B fiend, I used to have my nose up in the air when it came to rap music. Perhaps I was subliminally influenced by my judgmental grandfather, who associated rap music with danger and death. To his credit, he was no doubt influenced by N.W.A.'s takeover of Los Angeles. As an avid watcher of the five, six, and seven o'clock news (he'd be asleep by eight and awake by four a.m.), I'm sure the images of the gang violence in L.A. contributed to his distaste of and fear for what "that music" would do to his teenage grandsons. That fear rubbed off on my mother, which is part of the reason she insisted we pack up all our bags and leave for Senegal, which we did when I was four years old.

While the change of environment ensured that my brothers would never be in the crossfire of the notorious Bloods and Crips, it also put a huge delay on our access to American music. All I ever remember listening to in the late eighties was Michael Jackson, Senegalese music, the songs of Disney movie soundtracks, and "Take My Breath Away" from *Top Gun* (which I watched over and over again as a child).

After our stint in Africa, we moved back to the States, to Maryland, and it was the likes of Boyz II Men, Jade, Jodeci, SWV, and other R&B music that dominated the blissful nineties. My mom had an issue with the overt sexuality presented in some of the song lyrics, but I was too young to understand what they meant anyway. To this day, I still have no idea what my friends in elementary school were listening to back then, as I never had conversations about music with any of them. I was one of only a few black girls in the class and I had a naïve, childish perception that "black" music was for black people and "white" music was for white people, so it never occurred to me to talk about music with my friends. My mother, on the other hand, must have been having musical conversations with my friends' parents, because I don't know where else the idea for piano lessons could have come from. My best friend in elementary school, Lisa—a Jewish girl who invited me to her family's house for my very first Passover—took piano lessons. My mother, who'd always wanted to play the piano, thought it would be a great idea to place my younger brother and me in lessons as well. Besides, my great-grandmother's oak grand piano was just sitting in our living room, collecting dust (and random stickers, much to my mother's annoyance. "Who keeps putting stickers on the piano?!"). It was time to not only elevate her kids but also put the piano to use.

I was momentarily excited about the idea of playing the piano, if for no other reason than that my friend Lisa was doing it. My mother took us to a chic retail piano store in the Montgomery Mall—because all the piano greats took lessons in suburban malls—where we were taken to the back rooms of a piano retailer to meet Mr. Forbes, a heavy, happy spectacle-wearing man who, as I recall, looked like a young, curly-haired Philip Seymour Hoffman. He was my first real introduction to the piano, and his positive demeanor combined with a general optimism made me want to do well. He would instruct me for thirty minutes, after which I'd go next door to browse Sam Goody's music, while waiting for my brother to finish his session.

As our lessons with Mr. Forbes progressed, and I moved from Book One to Book Two of instruction, I also received a raise in my allowance from one dollar to two dollars a week. With my newly earned disposable income, I bought my very first tape single, Brandy's "I Wanna Be Down." I had owned a few tapes prior, most notably the soundtrack to Robert Townsend's *Meteor Man* and Raven-Symoné's first rap single, "That's What Little Girls Are Made Of" (which I later found out was produced by the brilliant Missy Elliott). Both of those tapes were picked out by me, but bought by my Tantie Rae. Brandy's single marked the first time I bought music with my own money, asserting my own fourth-grade independence. While my mother dropped us off for an hour at the mall every week, hoping that we'd learn the classics and develop skills to give us significant advantages as young black kids, she inadvertently granted me unsupervised musical autonomy, which I relished.

When Mr. Forbes moved away, much to my sadness, piano lessons were no longer exciting. Lisa's parents found another teacher and my mom found Ms. Wu, an older, hard-core, no-nonsense teacher whose highest compliment was "pwetty good, pwetty good." She got frustrated *so* easily! Because I work better with positive reinforcement, my desire to please her wasn't as high, and my mother had to force us to practice more than ever. This led to multiple crying sessions at the piano.

With tears and snot dripping on the keyboard, I distinctly remember yelling out, "I DON'T EVEN WANT TO DO THIS, MOM!"

And her, with unsympathetic eyes rolling infinitely, yelling back, "DO YOU KNOW HOW MANY PEOPLE WISH THEY COULD PLAY THE PIANO?! YOU WILL THANK ME WHEN YOU GET OLDER!"

I would get confirmations from my older brothers, who'd come back to town, impressed with our piano skills, feeling robbed of their own opportunities for piano lessons as kids. This satisfaction of having something they didn't would temporarily compel me to practice. But I was more motivated by our impending move to Los Angeles, which fueled my hopes that piano lessons would be in the days of Maryland past.

As luck would have it, our Los Angeles move placed us right across the street from a piano instructor: Ms. Harvey literally lived twelve footsteps away from our house. Now, there were no excuses as to why we couldn't go to lessons. No convincing my mother that she was too tired to take us. Nope. As my mother could now see the house of instruction from her living room window, she actually enforced mandatory daily practice sessions, using our manual oven timer to make sure we were moving our fingers for at least thirty minutes. It was all the more painful because we practiced in the extra cold or ridiculously hot living room also known as the "good" room, though the air didn't properly circulate. Piano practice interrupted television time, phone time, and even homework time.

"But Mom, I'm doing homework!"

"Do it after. It's only thirty minutes."

Thirty minutes felt like hours. Often, instead of sitting down and practicing my assigned song, I would listen for my mother's retreating footsteps, sneak to the kitchen, and turn the manual timer counterclockwise, deducting ten or fifteen minutes of practice time. The timer's buzz would signal a personal victory only if my mother wasn't listening. Sometimes, despite my committing to the allotted practice time, she would insist that I take more time.

"I didn't hear you playing the whole time. Do fifteen more minutes."

Maybe I was so hesitant to invest time because part of me knew that practicing didn't matter with Ms. Harvey. For one thing, Ms. Harvey was in her mid-eighties, at best. Secondly, while she demonstrated masterful skill on the piano (she once played at Carnegie Hall), her house smelled like dried pee, and she had to tend to her thirty-five-year-old daughter who had Down syndrome between hour-long sessions (that were supposed to be thirty minutes). Finally, Ms. Harvey suffered from Alzheimer's. Do you know what that means? That means that I played the same two Chopin songs for two years.

No matter how many times I complained to my mother about this, she remained sternly amused. "You're still learning. Just get really good at the songs you're learning, and now and then slip her a new song." But Ms. Harvey didn't want to play any of my songs. I slipped her the *Soul Food* soundtrack music book that I begged my

mother to buy, so that I could impress my friends with my knowledge of pop music. But, nope. "Too secular." I slipped her "People
Make the World Go Round," which I knew about only because Ice
Cube and the Westside Connection remade it as "Gangstas Make
the World Go Round." Turns out I underestimated the depth of her
oldness, because even that song didn't qualify as an "oldie" in her
book. Ms. Harvey was all about the classics, which I would learn to
respect later in life but hated in my years as a middle schooler.

Eventually, I resigned myself to the fact that my mother wasn't
going to let up on the piano-playing thing. So I tried to teach myself
popular, familiarly hip tunes on the piano. If I could get the party
jumping with "secular" tunes then, in my mind, I was guaranteed a
ticket into the cool crowd.

"Ay y'all, look what Jo-Issa can play on the piano!" they'd exclaim as they all gathered around me, Crip Walking and grinding
on the piano as I effortlessly prodded the keys and bounced to my
own tunes. Piano dancing always looks cool, and it was also a way
to mask what I couldn't do, dance. Who cares that you can't dance
when you can make music on the piano!

That never happened. I never got good enough to play multiple
songs at will. Not even when, after Ms. Harvey passed, we got a
new piano teacher, Mr. Wreath. I was in high school and Mr. Wreath
was cool, energetic, fun, and gay. He never brought up his sexuality,
but he didn't have to. He always talked about going to dance at the
Hollywood casino and about getting his "groove on" to his "jams"
with "people." He had a texturized S-curl and loved playing Gospel
music. My gaydar wasn't too keen in high school, but Mr. Wreath
was my first positive ID (I would get confirmation years later). He
was always excited to teach me the music I wanted to learn. With
him, I finally learned Boyz II Men's "A Song for Momma" off the

*Soul Food* soundtrack. I learned Gospel chords and melodious ar-
peggios and . . . that's about it. Because what my siblings and I loved
most about Mr. Wreath was how easy he was to sidetrack. That man
loved to talk. Sometimes we distracted him from noticing that we
hadn't practiced that week by asking him questions, the answers to
which he'd drag on and on about until our time was up. My mom
started to catch on and asked us if Mr. Wreath's talking was getting
in the way of our learning time. She didn't want to feel like she was
wasting her money. Oblivious to the money she was, in fact, wasting on this man, we'd innocently and deceitfully praise his teaching
methods. "He's so much better than Ms. Harvey."

We'd gotten so good at distracting Mr. Wreath that by the time
we approached our first recital, we weren't ready. At all. My mother
sat back and watched as we were the only kids who flubbed and
fumbled notes, pausing throughout our respective performances to
figure out which keys to play. The only thing more embarrassing
was that months later, Mr. Wreath dropped us as clients. He regret-
fully informed my mother that he was adding more clients to his
roster and had to focus on the ones that were taking piano seriously.
*Ouch.*

My embarrassment was short-lived, because my mom *finally*
stopped pressing us to play and came to the conclusion that forcing
us wasn't going to actually make us "good." Thankfully, my mother's years of piano investment wouldn't completely go to waste, as
my younger brother, Lamine, would grow up to produce music,
becoming better at the piano than I could ever have hoped to be.

I've always had my own musical ambitions. During the summer
before seventh grade, I decided to form a rap group. I was learning
how to make web pages, via Geocities and similar DIY home-page
designers, and I wanted to use these pages to market my group. I

mentioned to my best friend, Ashley, and her friend, London, a beautiful, ridiculously nice fourteen-year-old who'd just moved next door to her, that we should start a group and that I'd make our web pages. They were initially both bored by the idea until I asserted that it would be a great way to meet guys. With a laugh and a shrug, they decided to give it a shot. I designed our website, wrote a song verse for our first single, and even came up with our official group name: Star 69. The perfect combination of star power, pop culture, and sexual innuendo. I was a genius. Unfortunately, though, my group mates weren't very serious about their rap ambitions. The internet didn't appeal to them as a viable means of hip-hop fame and fortune, and so the group faded away.

By the time I left public school to enroll in Brentwood Middle School, I found my dad's stash of blank tapes. I started to record my favorite songs off the radio and discovered OHHLA.com, also known as the Original Hip-Hop Lyrics Archive. Whereas explicit words were bleeped from the radio, I read and learned them online. I still didn't really understand what they meant, but it was a step in the right direction. While I thought I was finally on par with my peers, some of my friends in the black clique I had befriended started getting into CDs and CD players. I desperately wanted to be a part of the conversation. That year for my Christmas wish list, I made sure to include a list of multiple CDs. I listed Ma$e's *Harlem World*, Janet Jackson's *The Velvet Rope*, Timbaland & Magoo's *Welcome to Our World*, Missy Elliott's *Supa Dupa Fly*, Boyz II Men's *Evolution*, and the new LSG (Levert Sweat Gill) album, because I vividly remember Keith Sweat's "Nobody" playing during the summer we moved to Los Angeles. His popularity could get me social points. Later I would realize that he was popular only in a certain young-mom demographic. Christmas morning I found three CDs: the ones by Boyz II Men, Janet, and LSG. Santa Claus had apparently decided that the CDs with "Parental Advisory" labels were naughty. (Though through several listens, I found that Janet Jackson was *pret-ty* naughty.)

I had given up on trying to get CDs through my mother, but my birthday was coming up that January and I decided to throw a party with some of my girlfriends. "No boys allowed," my mother conditioned. How absolutely lame! Jennifer, my friend from A Better Chance, an organization for kids from diverse socioeconomic and racial backgrounds attending prep school, had just thrown her own birthday house party. Her mother not only allowed boys, but set up the living room for her daughter and her friends to freak dance. That's love.

I was so easily impressed by the freedom and the general semblance of a high school party that it never occurred to me that her party might be "wack." I mean, who was I—awkward, socially hungry—to deem a party uncool or lame? But that was the general sentiment when we returned to school that Monday: Jennifer's party was wack. If her party, with boys and dancing and nighttime fun, was declared a failure socially, then did my party really have a chance? I should have rescinded any thoughts I had about having a party at that moment, but my mother was insistent. She thought it would be fun for me and wanted to meet all my friends. "I'll even hire a clown for you and your little friends," she offered, cracking herself up, while I searched her eyes in horror.

My "friends" arrived, prepared to be bored. All except Cherie, who remained optimistic. We sat in the living room as I tried to encourage conversation, which worked for a while until Amber, Jennifer's best friend who was a year older, started talking about *Friday*—her favorite movie of all time.

I seized my opportunity to brag, "My cousins made *Friday*."

Their eyes widened. "Ice Cube is your cousin?!"

"No . . . He made it with my cousins."

"Oh. Do you have it? We could watch that instead of just sitting here."

This was the most excited I had seen them all night. I had to deliver, though I had never even seen *Friday* because my mother still wouldn't let me watch R-rated movies. The living room housed a closet full of hundreds of videotapes—home movies and commercial movies alike. My friends gathered around me as I tried to find *Friday*. Amber grabbed a tape. "Y'all got *Player's Club*, too? Ooo!" I told them my cousins had made that movie, too.

"Your cousins made all my favorite movies." (In hindsight, that this middle schooler's favorite movies were centered around weed and strip clubs makes me sad.)

As they pressured me to take them to the TV room so I could immediately redeem my party, I sighed, knowing what I had to do.

I went to the kitchen, where my mom was slicing my party pizza into thinner slices.

"Mom, they really want to watch *Friday*. Can we?"

"Unh-unh. You know you can't."

"But Mom, Cousin Pat and Michael made it. Our family! And everyone wants to watch it. PLEASE?!"

"No. Find something else to watch."

"Can we watch *Player's Club*?"

"*Player's Club*? Absolutely not. That's even worse."

"But Mom, nobody's having any fun. Please, Mom, I don't want my party to suck."

My mom turned to face me. Did I sense a gleam of sympathy?

"Find something else to watch. There are hundreds of tapes in there."

I wanted to sink my head into my soft, square-shaped shell of a body and disappear. This was it. I was going to solidify my position as the loser of the group. I turned away from my mother, stiffly, ready to resign myself to that position. I broke the news and the girls looked at me, stunned. Jennifer rolled her eyes. Cherie's permanent smile wavered. Amber looked at me incredulously.

"So that means you haven't even seen *Friday*?"

We moved to the bedroom my little sister and I shared, where I sat on my bunk bed as I opened my gifts. Jennifer handed me hers in a small gift bag. I was excited just to receive a present from her. I threw the tissue paper to the side and looked inside. It was the Ma$e album! I was ecstatic, my eyes instantly darting around the room for a place to hide it from my mother.

"Thank you so much! I can't believe you got this for me!"

Jennifer shrugged. "Someone gave me an extra one for my birthday, so . . ."

I didn't care that I was re-gifted. This was my first "explicit" album. I was so ready. Then, Amber (who hadn't gotten me a gift) took out her own CD, Lil' Kim's *Hard Core* album, shifting the conversation. Everybody talked about how nasty and raw the album was as she popped the CD into my boom box. I didn't have any expectations, though just looking at the album cover with Lil' Kim in a full-on squat, legs open—literally "taking pictures," as my Southern aunts used to say—should have been a warning.

It was on this album that I heard the sound of a vagina being "eaten." Something I didn't know, up until that point, could be done. I turned it off quickly, horrified that my mother would walk in, and the girls were, at last, understanding. Then the conversation shifted to talking about our personal sexual experiences and/or lack thereof. I decided I was too young to hear that album in its entirety. I was kind of offended and embarrassed that Lil' Kim was so explicit. Maybe my mother was right to shield me from that kind of music. But that didn't mean I was going to throw out my Ma$e CD. Owning the CD finally allowed me to contribute to the conversations I'd been missing out on around the proverbial water cooler, i.e. the vending machine. It broadened my social life, opened a door that I didn't want to close.

I was so desperate not to close it that, weeks later, I constructed a web of lies about my "music collection" that later came to bite me in the ass. Courtney, Allison's older sister and the leader of our lunchtime group (a group comprised of the only black kids in the school, minus a few "Ambitious Blacks"; see "ABG Guide: Connecting with Other Blacks"), proposed throwing a lunchtime party in our designated spot, under the shady tree of the school's roundabout. She had already begun a trend of pooling our money once a month and ordering Domino's pizza. If you didn't bring your money, you didn't get pizza. So she suggested having a mini party with pizza and music. We were talking about the music we were feeling: Dru Hill's *Enter the Dru*; Puff Daddy's *No Way Out*; Missy's *Supa Dupa Fly*; and the Timbaland & Magoo, Aaliyah, and Ginuwine squad that accompanied her—and something possessed me to claim that I owned all those albums. She turned to me.

"For real? All of them?"

"Well . . . some of them are my older brothers', but basically."

Courtney and Allison exchanged glances. Then Courtney asked, "Can you bring them? If you bring them on Friday, I can have a mix made over the weekend and bring it to the lunch party."

My heart dropped. "Yeah. For sure."

Courtney grew excited. "This party is 'bout to be so tight."

They resumed talking about whatever as my head swirled, thinking about how I'd obtain access to *one* of these CDs, much less all of them. My allowance had increased to five dollars a week, but I had poor spending habits and no inclination to save for potential self-imposed emergencies. Why was the ownership of the music that people cherished so important to me? Why did I feel the need to fabricate an elaborate collection? Did I want people to like me that badly? Had I the tech prowess necessary then, I surely would have been the first to create Napster, which burst on the scene just a year later.

I went to school the following day, the day before my Friday deadline, hoping Courtney had forgotten about my claims. No such luck. When lunchtime came around she greeted me excitedly.

"You're bringing the CDs tomorrow, right?"

"Yeah. I meant to bring them today. But tomorrow, for sure."

"Cool. Jennifer and Cherie. Y'all are bringing yours, too, right?"

"Yup," exclaimed Cherie and Jennifer, simultaneously, between chews.

"Great. We're set. Don't forget the money for the pizza, too."

WHO THE HELL RAISED HER TO BE SO DAMN RESPONSIBLE?! (That responsibility would eventually lead her successfully into and through med school, but who's keeping track?) I wanted time to stand still. I wanted a major distraction to make everyone forget my promise. But I had no luck. I sat at home, trying to figure out what I could do to soften the blow of not making good on a promise. Then it hit me.

I stayed my ass home from school. I convinced my mother that I was sick. It was the perfect plan. Missing school on Friday would give me the entire weekend for them to forget about my nondelivery. Sure, the party was the coming Monday, but at least I wouldn't have to fess up to my lie. The mix CD would already be made, the pizza would already be ordered, and my reputation would be blemished, but not tarnished.

As predicted, that Monday I was passive-aggressively ostracized, as I tried to play up how bad my sudden weekend sickness was. More than ever, I needed to find a way to redeem myself, musically.

One day, I was perusing a *Vibe* magazine issue (back when Mimi Valdés, whom I would later work with, was the editor-in-chief), and I came across the Columbia House/BMG ads that were generously inserted throughout music magazines. The advertisement stated that you could get twelve CDs for the price of one cent. This was absolutely within my price range, so it must have been too good to be true. I gave it a shot anyway, perusing their catalogue, picking out CDs that I wanted or had heard my friends discussing. I didn't get any "Parental Advisory" CDs, for fear of my mother discovering and opening the package before me. I was only thirteen, so I didn't have a credit card or a checkbook, but luckily, they had a "Bill Me Later" option. I was tempted to include a penny in the envelope but didn't want to chance it falling out.

Luckily, the day the package arrived, I was home. I opened it and saw the holy grail of nineties music in front of me: 112's *Room 112*, Brandy's *Never Say Never*, Dru Hill's *Enter the Dru*, Lauryn Hill's *The Miseducation of Lauryn Hill*, Brandy and Monica's *The Boy Is Mine*, and Mýa's self-titled debut album. Six CDs were more than I had ever owned at once. Apparently they gave you six CDs to start and expected payment before they sent the other six. The bill was definitely more than a penny, so I had no intentions of paying it. I can proudly say that I had my first and only black mark on my credit when I was thirteen years old. Thanks for teaching me the value of a penny, BMG!

When I turned sixteen, one year shy of the "Parental Advisory" age restriction, my mother was kind enough to allow me to finally see R-rated movies. Since I was driving by that time, she probably figured that I was going to see them anyway. She was right. I don't know why I didn't break the rules sooner. Maybe I was content with being shielded from certain adult themes. After all, I do remember being a high school junior and wanting to wait until marriage to lose my virginity. I laugh at that notion now. Innocence after elementary school is so contrived.

When I got to high school, sex took on another dimension, one beyond what I could glimpse in explicit lyrics and videos. High school was also where I was exposed to the 'hood in all its glory. I was a fascinated outsider, simultaneously wanting to belong, but to not be included. Everybody wants to be hood, but nobody *really* wants to be hood.

In the post-Luke era, high school is also where music started to get exceptionally raunchy. I remember such gems as "I Just Wanna F*** You" and Ludacris's debut single, "What's Your Fantasy," where, during a lunch dance, a bunch of fourteen-year-old students happily yelled out the bridge while popping their pelvises and asses:

*I wanna get you in the BACK SEAT,*

*Windows up,*

*That's the way,*

*YOU LIKE TO @&\*$!*

High school is also where I gave my music ambitions another shot. My sophomore year, I got Mr. E for Chemistry. He was Persian, had med school ambitions, and lots of money (but wanted to "give back" via Teach for America), and was one of the coolest teachers ever. We were the envy of the school when he decided to take all his Chemistry classes to Magic Mountain that year—for

NO REASON! It was in Mr. E's second-period class that I grew close to many of my current friends, but most importantly, where I formed HOC-D (pronounced "Hawk-DUH!"). The group was comprised of three of the prettiest girls from my high school (two of whom became models, one of whom was a top-three finalist on *America's Next Top Model*) . . . and me. Daisy, who took it absolutely seriously, is one of my current friends. She was born and raised in Compton, was super smart (ranked #11 in our class at graduation), was a talented dancer, never stressed about guys (because she didn't have to and they sweated *her*), and like me, she loved the music of the hoodrats. The day we formed HOC-D, which was an acronym of our last names, she wrote verses to two songs that night. While HOC-D never amounted to much, Daisy's dedication to the art form of ratchetry would always stick with me, even when we went away to different colleges.

Despite going to school in Compton—the breeding ground of gangsta rap, and the source of inspiration for many rappers—it wasn't until I attended Stanford that my ratchet aspirations were truly nurtured. In the middle of Palo Alto, I met three girls who enabled me. One night over a series of drunken freestyle sessions my senior year of college, we formed JAM'D (an acronym of our first names—I wasn't very creative with titles). I got the idea to record our session on my computer and then created a picture collage on Windows Media Maker of our first freestyle single, "@&*$You, Bitch." It was my very first YouTube video and my very first music "hit" (the YouTube video would go on to amass over 150,000 views). Our peers loved the song and loved the video. We'd go on to create three more singles: "Nani Pop," a dance dedicated to female pelvic thrusts; "Catakilla," an angry gangsta anthem about murdering the caterpillars that infested our campus; and "Working the V," a song about vaginal attention (promptly made private after my eldest brother commented on the video).

After I graduated and moved to New York, my musical ambitions took a hiatus, due to lack of enablers. All my friends were too busy taking their careers seriously while I was still trying to figure myself out. But my desire never went away. In fact, the discovery that my younger brother's music group, Fly Guys, had gained a bit of internet fame due to a popular dance group using their song in a video actually helped to restore my hope for a musical future. When I moved back to Los Angeles after a two-year stint in New York, making a music video for the Fly Guys was one of my first projects. Between their lyrics, their stage presence, and their dedication, I learned a lot from them.

In Los Angeles, I was also reunited with my best friends from high school. In the summer of 2009, before I returned to Senegal, Jerome, Devin, and Daisy (my fellow HOC-D alum) were joking around in our Facebook messages and decided to throw a party at my mother's house and invite all our mutual friends. It was my L.A. homecoming party, and it was also the formation of the Doublemint Twins (now known as The Doublemints). That same summer, a group trip to Magic Mountain and an accompanying heat wave prompted us to start singing, "That's why we got on our booty shawts, booty shawts!" So pleased with ourselves, we vowed we would make that our first single. Around the same time, the first episode of *Awkward Black Girl* was still stewing in my head. By the time I figured out what the opening scene was going to be, I knew I wanted to include a raunchy song. While I initially envisioned a Nicki Minaj song, when we sat down and actually recorded our lyrics on my computer, I was inspired to make it the opening song of my first episode. A week before I premiered the first episode, we recorded the single in the Fly Guys garage-based studio and boom, magic was made.

Even with my love for ratchet music, I've always had a fear of what my children will be listening to in the future, when they are in middle school. I have a preemptive desire to shield them from sex for as long as possible and to protect their innocence as my parents did for me. I joke with a college friend of mine, Adia, who had the same parental restrictions as I did, that we will raise our kids around one another. We agree that friends make all the difference in the exposure you have and the life choices you make. I don't regret meeting any of my friends, and I don't regret my generation's affinity for ratchet music. And, while my high school and college reunions will contain the raunchiest soundtracks, I won't ever bring that shit home to my future kids.

# The Struggle

I don't remember the exact day I demilitarized from my blackness. It's all a blur and since I'm fairly certain that militants never forget, and I forget stuff *all* the time, I guess I wasn't meant to be one.

I love being black; that's not a problem. The problem is that I don't want to always *talk* about it because honestly, talking about being "black" is extremely tiring. I don't know how Al Sharpton and Jesse Jackson do it. I know why Cornel West and Tavis Smiley do it. They *love* the attention and the groupies. But the rest of these people who talk, think, and breathe race every single day—how? Just how? Aren't they exhausted?

The pressure to contribute to these conversations now that we have a black president is even more infuriating.

"What do you think about what's going on in the world? And how our black president is handling it?" asks a race baiter.

"It's all good, I guess," I want to answer, apathetically, with a

Kanye shrug. "I'm over it." But am I really? Could I be even if I wanted to?

Even now, I feel obligated to write about race. It's as though it's expected of me to acknowledge what we all already know. The truth is, I slip in and out of my black consciousness, as if I'm in a racial coma. Sometimes, I'm so deep in my anger, my irritation, my need to stir change, that I can't see anything outside of the lens of race.

At other times I feel guilty about my apathy. But then I think, *isn't this what those who came before me fought for?* The right *not* to have to deal with race? If faced with a choice between fighting until the death for freedom and civil rights and living life without any acknowledgment of race, they'd choose the latter.

Growing up as a young black girl in Potomac, Maryland, was easy. I never really had to put much thought into my race, and neither did anybody else. I had a Rainbow Coalition of friends of all ethnicities, and we would carelessly skip around our elementary school like the powerless version of Captain Planet's Planeteers. I knew I was black. I knew there was a history that accompanied my skin color and my parents taught me to be proud of it. End of story.

All that changed when my family moved to Los Angeles and placed me in a middle school where my blackness was constantly questioned—and not even necessarily in the traditional sense, i.e. "You talk white, Oreo girl" or "You can't dance, white girl." Those claims were arguable, for the most part. My biggest frustration in the challenge to prove my "blackness" usually stemmed from two very annoying, very repetitive situations:

SITUATION #1: "I'm not even black, and I'm blacker than you." It's one thing when other African Americans try to call me out on my race card, but when people outside my ethnicity have the audacity to question how "down" I am because of the bleak, stereotypical picture pop culture has painted of black women, it's a whole other thing. Unacceptable. I can recall a time when I was having a heated discussion with a white, male classmate of mine. Our eighth-grade class was on a museum field trip as the bus driver blasted Puff Daddy's "Been Around the World" to drown us out.

It began as a passive competition of lyrics, as we each silently listened for who would mess up first. By the second verse, our lazy rap-whispers escalated to an aggressive volume, accompanied by rigorous side-eyes by the time we got to, "Playa please, I'm the macaroni with the cheese," and I felt threatened. Was this fool seriously trying to outrap me? And why did I care? After the song ended, he offered his opinion: "Puff Daddy is wack, yo." How dare he? Not only was I pissed, but I felt as if he had insulted my own father (who did I think I was? Puff Daughter?).

"Puff Daddy is tight," I retorted. He rolled his eyes and said, "Have you heard of [insert Underground rapper]? Now, *he's* dope." I hadn't heard of him, but I couldn't let this white boy defeat me in rap music knowledge, especially as others started to listen. "Yeah, I know him. He's not dope," I lied, for the sake of saving face. Perhaps because he saw through me or because he actually felt strongly about this particular artist, he asked me to name which songs I thought were "not dope." Panic set in as I found myself exposed, then—"You don't even know him, huh? Have you even heard of [insert Random Underground rapper]?"

As he continued to rattle off the names of make-believe-sounding MCs, delighted that he had one-upped me, he managed to make me feel as though my credibility as a black person relied on my knowledge of hip-hop culture. My identity had been reduced to the Bad Boy label clique as this boy seemingly claimed my black card as his own.

Of course, as I grew older and Ma$e found his calling as a reverend, I realized there was more to being black than a knowledge of rap music, and that I didn't have to live up to this pop cultural archetype. I began to take pride in the fact that I couldn't be reduced to a stereotype and that I didn't have to be. This leads me to my next situation:

SITUATION #2: "Black people don't do that." Or so I'm told by a black person. These, too, are derived from (mostly negative) stereotypes shaped by popular culture. The difference is that in these situations, we black people are the ones buying into these stereotypes.

When I was a teenager, for example, others questioned my blackness because some of the life choices I made weren't considered to be "black" choices: joining the swim team when it is a known fact that "black people don't swim," or choosing to become a vegetarian when blacks clearly love chicken. These choices and the various positive and negative responses to them helped to broaden my own perspective on blackness and, eventually, caused me to spurn these self-imposed limitations. But not before embarrassing the hell out of myself in a poor attempt to prove I was "down." I'll never forget submitting a school project in "Ebonics" for my seventh-grade English class, just to prove that I could talk *and* write "black." I was trying to prove it to myself just as much as I was to everyone around me.

Even in my early adulthood, post-college, I'd overtip to demonstrate I was one of the good ones. Only recently have I come to ask, *What am I trying to prove and to whom am I proving it?* Today, I haven't completely rid myself of the feeling that I'm still working through Du Bois's double consciousness.

For the majority of my life I cared too much about how my blackness was perceived, but *now?* At this very moment? I couldn't care less. Call it maturation or denial or self-hatred—I give no f%^&s. And it feels great. I've decided to focus only on the positivity of being black, and especially of being a black woman. Am I supposed to feel oppressed? Because I don't. Is racism supposed to hurt me? That's so 1950s. Should I feel marginalized? I prefer to think of myself as belonging to an "exclusive" club.

While experiencing both types of situations—being made to feel not black enough by "down" white people on one hand and not black enough by the blacks in the so-called know on the other—has played a role in shaping a more comfortably black me, in the end, I have to ask: Who is to say what we do and don't do? What we can and can't do? The very definition of "blackness" is as broad as that of "whiteness," yet the media seemingly always tries to find a specific, limited definition. As CNN produces news specials about us, and white and Latino rappers feel culturally dignified in using the N-word, our collective grasp of "blackness" is becoming more and elusive. And that may not be a bad thing.

# Halfrican

Growing up post–*Coming to America* had some benefits. For one, the 1988 film helped to counter the stereotypical, impoverished, *National Geographic* images of Africa that so many were used to seeing at that time. Ironically, the year prior, Eddie Murphy's own comedy special, *Raw*, had helped to perpetuate the notion of uncivilized Africans. Mfufu, with the bone in her nose, formerly "butt naked on a zebra" suddenly expressed her dissatisfaction with the economic inequality of their relationship, "Ed-die, why you treat me like animaux?"

*Coming to America* brought on a shift in dumb questions, from "Oh you're from Africa—do you hunt lions?" to "Oh, you're from Africa—is your family royalty?" I didn't have any African friends outside of family until I went to high school. Even then, the many Nigerians there didn't flaunt their African ancestry, and I wasn't included in their clique because I wasn't one of them.

In my French class, I met a girl named Monique from Zaire who, like me, already spoke French and was taking the class to get an

easy "A." More advanced in her French than I was, she knew all
the French slang and spoke in the tone of a peppy Valley girl. She
seemed to relish the opportunity to secretly talk shit about our peers
in French. "*Le gars la est trop con,*" she'd exclaim to me with a smile
in a sweet tone that suggested we were discussing flowers and candy.

And we became fast friends when she found out I was from
Senegal.

"Oh my God, the guys in Senegal are *so* cute!"

———

The first time I ever felt beautiful was when I went back to Senegal,
my sophomore year of high school. It was the first time I had boys
and men pining after me. As a moderate feminist, I shouldn't rely
on the validation of men to feel a sense of worth, but as I mentioned, it was high school, so stop judging. Initially, I convinced
myself that all of this sudden attention was because I had lived in
America. I wasn't naïve to the fact that many Senegalese men saw
foreign women as an opportunity to "escape," to establish a better
life abroad. Americans were particularly coveted, back when the
dollar meant a damn. Before euros emerged as the desired currency,
everyone wanted to go to the States. Even people who swore they
hated America wanted a piece of it, somehow, some way. I took this
into account whenever I was hit on, or whenever I was proposed to,
or whenever men offered to impregnate me—you know, the usual.

European and American women of all shapes, sizes, and facial
structures were shamelessly courted by Senegalese men of varying
beauty, so I knew not to take their attention too seriously. In some
sense, we were all like the hefty, juicy chicken mirages seen only by
the hungry, thirsty stragglers lost in the desert, fantasizing about
survival. But whatevs—I finally experienced what it meant to feel

beautiful. And part of me denied that I was in the same category as those other women, because I was part Senegalese. I was a product of their generational loins, indirectly.

Superficial reasons aside, my other "feelings of beauty" stemmed from the interactions I had with my Senegalese family, whom I hadn't seen since elementary school. I was on the brink of womanhood now, and I had a new appreciation for them. One particular cousin, Ndeye Awa, is someone I've looked up to since childhood. With smooth ebony skin and sculpted features, she is absolutely beautiful. The running joke among the family is that she's "too skinny," but there was always a general consensus that she could come to the States and be a model, easily. She and her older sister, Lissa, who was closer in age to my older brother, were the absolute coolest. Lissa was what the Senegalese call *claire* (literally: "clear," meaning light-skinned, which by Senegalese standards meant her skin was copper-colored). Curvy and very beautiful, she could have had her pick of men. To know that I was related to these two alone already instilled in me a sense of pride. But when I returned the summer before my tenth-grade year, and was reunited with all of my aunts, my first cousins, and some of my first cousins' children under the roof of the family patriarch, I was overwhelmed with happiness. This was *my* family.

We had actually moved to Senegal as a family when I was three years old. My dad felt that we needed to learn more discipline and my mother was worried about what the budding Los Angeles gang violence would mean for her three sons, then aged twelve, ten, and a few months. As a toddler, I had no qualms about the move, but for my older brothers, it was the end of the world. Amadou and Malick had friends and reputations they were leaving behind in the only city they knew. They were devastated, which is probably why their love affair with Senegal is, to this day, a bit tenuous. I had no idea about anything life had to offer, so the adaptation was fairly easy for me. Senegalese food? Bring it on. Wolof and French? Guess I'm trilingual up in here!

Yes, my parents were ready to start a new life in Senegal, leaving the States behind for good. During the time we spent there, we had a great life. We lived in a huge, multilevel house, with a security guard and two maids, in an affluent area called Anne Mariste. I could see my cousins whenever I wanted to and was in a school where my American-ness made me special. Life was great, for two years. Until my father attempted to build a hospital in Senegal and instead got ripped off by the government, losing most of his money in the process. That's when, to my sadness and my older brothers' relief, we packed our bags to return to the States.

We wouldn't come back to visit until I was ten years old and, while that visit served as a brief reminder of what once was, it didn't trigger any fond nostalgia. In fact, during that particular visit, the one thing I took back with me was "Roachelle," a cruel nickname given to me by my mother on the plane ride back home. One of my only surface gripes with Senegal, due to several horrible experiences and really, the general grossness of them, is the abundance of cockroaches. If you don't see them, they're somewhere. The incident that sparked my new nickname began at the Dakar airport, on our way back home to Potomac, Maryland. I really had to use the restroom and couldn't wait until we got past the ticketing line to go. I was wearing an all-white *booboo*, with beautiful color-printed accents, and these cute white harem pants. The outfit was a parting gift from a relative that my mother insisted, to demonstrate our appreciation, I put on right away.

My family waited for me in the ticketing area as I pee-pee danced to the bathroom. As soon as I walked inside, I knew I didn't want to be in there for very long. It smelled like a urine fairy was floating around the bathroom, blowing his pee-pee breath ever-so-delicately directly up my nostrils. I rushed inside the stall and pulled down my pants, only to look down and see several small roaches scurrying along the floor tiles. I quickly pulled my pants up to my thighs, holding them tightly while keeping balanced enough to squat over the seatless toilet, all the while attempting to keep my eye on every single roach, to ensure my safety. When I got out of the restroom, before I could tell my mother about the nastiness, she rushed us to the gate.

In the middle of the thirteen-hour plane ride back home, I kept feeling a strange brushing sensation on my inner thigh. Being a stupid child, apparently too lazy to investigate unfamiliar sensations, I ignored the tingling the first three times it occurred. Maybe the cloth in my new pants was especially stringy in the crotch area? After the fourth brush-up, I reached down and discovered a hole right in the center of my pants. Intrigued, I stuck my hand near my inner thigh to see what was causing my irritation. I grabbed what I thought was a loose piece of fabric or a tag, held it to my face for closer inspection, and was met with the absolutely disgusting cycling legs of a thick, three-inch-long cockroach. I freaked the entire hell out and instinctively threw it out of my hands, next to me, where my younger brother sat. Horrified, he let out a high-pitched squeal and brushed it off his chest and sent it flying down to the aisle between him and my mother, where it landed on its pedaling feet. My mother, who sat holding a four-year-old Elize, looked at the walking roach and shrieked with alarm. As it made its way to the front of the plane, my mother tapped the man sitting in front of her, who was engaged in reading a newspaper, and asked him with pleading panicked politeness, *"Monsieur,* could you please kill that roach?"

In response, the man barely turned his eyes to the floor, where the roach leisurely roamed, and calmly told her, "No." He resumed his newspaper reading as the roach prepared for his new life in New York, and *that's* the story of how "Roachelle" was almost impregnated by a cockroach.

———

In general, my mother and father have always been very good about keeping some aspect of Senegal in our lives, whether they intended to or not. One incident particularly endeared me to that culture. Alioune was one of my aunt Mame Bineta's friends and one of the many Senegalese visitors over the years who had extended his stay in our home. My mother quickly learned that when she said "I do" to my father, she said "I do" to his culture, which states that any visitor is welcome to stay at your house, eat your food, and cause you inconvenience, indefinitely—family or not. Many relatives took advantage of my dad's generosity and general politeness. In addition to sponsoring the visits of over fifty relatives and close family friends, my father has repeatedly housed at least half of them.

Alioune had been in our Los Angeles home for only a couple of days when, during a balcony smoke break, he saw what appeared to be a black baby doll floating on top of our backyard pool. Upon closer inspection, he realized it was my unconscious body and promptly ran down to jump in the pool and retrieve me. At only one and a half years old, I had wandered outside alone and fallen into the gateless pool. My mother called the paramedics in a frenzy as my brothers rushed outside to watch while Alioune administered CPR to me. Had it not been for a random Senegalese stranger staying at our house, I would certainly be dead.

This is a fact I'm sure my mother never forgot, and that must have remained in her mind as she tolerated more and more stays from visitors over the years, even after she and my father divorced.

One of our visitors, Cherif, my father's elderly "uncle" who resembled an African Redd Foxx, had decided to grace us with his presence for several weeks. I was fourteen at the time, and my parents and siblings were gone for some inexplicable reason. Maybe I had stayed home from school. Who knows? All I know is that I found myself alone with this man, who had to be in his seventies, but was still in good enough form to do some jumping jacks if he needed to. His French was broken and often unintelligible, and so was my Wolof, so our language barrier was pretty prominent. When he called me from my snack searching in the kitchen to where he lay stretched out on the couch, lazy and entitled, like the Senegalese version of Jabba the Hutt, I knew I'd be in for a struggle.

The request started out simple enough. He indicated his hands and asked me in a French-Wolof hybrid, "*Ana coupé? Coupé?*" (Literally: "Where's cut? Cut?")

It took me a minute, but all I had to do was look at his nails to understand his request.

"*Ahh, les couples d'ongles? Je vais les chercher.*" I pointed behind me and pronounced it again, louder, as if my volume would magically make him understand, "*CHERCHER!*"

So I went to find the nail clippers, which I knew my mother kept in some cluttered drawer of her bathroom. As I thoroughly searched each drawer, I crossed my fingers that we had all been responsible and considerate enough to have put them back where we found them. I shuffled through tampons and cotton balls and nail polish and . . . *Eureka!* I jogged back to the family room and handed them to him. He nodded with mild appreciation as he took them from me. I went back to my dad's office to internet surf.

Ten minutes later, my surfing was interrupted.

"Isseu!" Had I heard my name? I waited. Maybe he was coughing.

"Isseu!" Nope. Not a cough. I scooted away from my leisurely act of nothingness and made my way back to the family room. Cherif handed me the clippers and as I nodded, readying to put them back, he stopped me.

"*Xadda, xadda . . .*" I turned back to see him pointing, this time . . . at his feet. I looked down at the long-nailed toes he wiggled as he continued to say something in Wolof that I didn't *want* to understand. I tried to hand the nail clippers back to him and was met instead with a closed fist and single finger pointing in my direction. *Me?*

I played dumb. "*Quest-ce que tu veux?*"

More Wolof from him, then the word, "*coupe,*" as he made room for me on the couch, flexing his feet and pointing his toes.

I couldn't believe this mess. I didn't know what to do. I knew what I *didn't* want to do, but if I refused, would that be a grave sign of disrespect? Would I cause some family drama between him and my father? Or a confrontation of some sort? On the other hand, if I *did* do it, wouldn't I be disrespecting myself? Why did I have to be the only one home today? Why did this jerk feel so comfortable asking me to perform this task? At fourteen, did I look like someone who did man feet? Why couldn't I have been one of those roughneck Latina girls I went to high school with, who constantly disrespected authority figures without any remorse? ("I ain't doin' *dick*! F!@# yo' toes!")

I was far too polite and I hated that about myself. I didn't even know where to start. So, without touching his feet, I slowly started with the big toe. His feet weren't completely ugly, which I appreciated, but neither were they nice-looking enough to change my perspective on the matter.

*Clip.*

I looked at Cherif, who checked his toe. I guess that was good enough for him. He lay back and allowed me to continue. On to the next.

*C-lip. C-lip.* I felt my dignity and pride chip away with each nail that dropped to the towel he'd set below his feet. By the time I got to the fourth toe, which was kind of small, I tried to position the nail clipper just over the nail without putting his skin in the danger zone, and again without putting my hands on his feet. I could feel Cherif tense up, which made my hands shake out of nervousness and insecurity, which was enough for him to hold his hand up and say, "*Ça va. Ça va.*" We both exhaled as I gave him the clippers, and he finished the rest of the job himself. I didn't know what was worse, being asked to cut his toenails in the first place or being stopped because I wasn't doing a good enough job.

Fortunately, all of our other houseguests were far more considerate. Sure, we'd be relegated to sleeping in the living room as our beds were given away, but that inconvenience was mostly left to Lamine, who had his own room (Elize and I shared a room). Many of our guests would cook us delicious Senegalese food, give us rides to places we needed to go (including school), and do the chores we didn't want to do: *dishes.*

Up until my high school trip back to Dakar, practicing French with our guests by way of pleasant conversation and eating *Thiebou dien* and *Yassa* was enough to make me feel like I was still in touch with my culture. But, within the first day of my visit, I realized how wrong I was and how much I'd been missing out on, first and foremost, camaraderie with family.

One thing that had remained constant since we lived there when I was very young was the family house, the structure of which was unlike any other house I had ever seen, much less lived in. It resembled a single-story motel, in that there was a courtyard terrace with rooms surrounding it. The pathway at the entrance of the house led to an outdoor center terrace, off of which was a kitchen on the right, and then a family room. Most of our quality time was spent in one of two rooms, the family/living room (which held the youthful portraits of my grandparents) and my Tantie Ndeye Fatou's room, which held one of the bigger televisions in the house and a VCR.

We came with suitcases bearing many gifts, piled on by some of our aunts back in Los Angeles for their children, and medicine for my grandfather, but I'd say the most coveted item we held was the compilation of music videos I had recorded over the course of a week before we arrived. Before international internet, American music hits didn't come to Senegal until six months to a year later. What I held in my hand was pop culture currency, and the opportunity for my cousins to be ahead of the curve in their social circles. We must have watched those music videos every other day that summer, emulating the dances of Nelly and the St. Lunatics, learning all the lyrics to Ray J and Lil' Kim's "Wait A Minute" and rewatching the same Freestyle Friday battle on AJ and Free's *106 & Park*. Later, I'd find out that none of the songs I had recorded would be huge hits in the United States (so much for my A&R career), but they were mega hits around the house.

It was, perhaps, during one of these bored bouts of rewatching music videos that I expressed a desire to go out and do something fun.

"Do you want to go to the club?" my cousin, Pape Amadou,[7] asked.

*The club?* Did they know I was only fifteen?

"I'm only fifteen," I suggested.

P'Amadou, who was seventeen, shrugged. "That doesn't matter. You can get into the clubs at sixteen here—they don't care."

I had yet another brief moment of panic as I considered my inability to dance, but then I realized I was among family. Plus, the club would probably be playing mostly Senegalese music anyway, and I wasn't expected to know how to do those moves.

"Niani plays really good rap and R&B," he added.

*Oh.* Well, still . . . I was among family, and why not?

"Let's go!" I exclaimed.

We took two cabs to Niani. P'Amadou rode with some of his neighborhood guy friends in one cab, and I rode with Skinny Ndeye Awa and my older cousin Khady in another cab. I had "dressed up" in my Nike Prestos (shoes that were the envy of all my guy cousins), blue jeans that I had rolled up to the ankle, a red tank top, and a red bandanna that blew in the wind as I sat in the backseat, by the window. I looked like I was auditioning to be a Jet in *West Side Story*, but I thought I was cute.

We got inside the club at around ten o'clock, and it was nearly empty. As we took seats at one of the many vacant booths, DJ

---

7 Yes, I have a brother named Amadou *and* about ten cousins named Amadou. My grandfather's name is also Amadou. I have a brother named Malick, and I have about ten cousins named Malick. Both names are like the equivalent of John and James, respectively.

Eduardo played a song by a Brit named Craig David that I had never heard before, "Walking Away." Craig David had released only one song in the United States that I'd heard, called "Fill Me In." The Senegalese were way more familiar with him than we were. I bobbed to the song as I took it all in, the fancily lit dance floor and the adult ambience that made up the décor. By the time eleven thirty hit, the club started to fill up with teens and adults in their twenties, alike. My cousins and I hit the dance floor, with P'Amadou busting the "Big Pimpin'" dance at every opportunity. I was enjoying myself immensely, dancing in a way that felt comfortable, which consisted mostly of upper-body and hand movements.

I was mid–hand dance when I caught the eye of a tall, dark, handsomely thuggish-ruggish-bone-looking guy who was watching me dance. I looked away and continued dancing near Ndeye Awa, who by then expressed that she was ready to sit down with Khady, who at twenty-six was acting closer to forty-six. I told her to go have a seat without me, as I was still dancing with P'Amadou and his friends. I looked back at Thuggish-Ruggish, who continued to look my way and smiled. Now confident that he was actually looking at me, I smiled, nodded back, then turned away and waited. As I started feeling the music and myself a little bit more, I turned back to see a shorter, darker, nicely-dressed-but-not-who-I-was-looking-for gentleman come my way, smiling. He started dancing in front of me, mimicking my dance moves, making them look way cooler. I smiled, impressed, and we continued to dance as I looked around for Thuggish-Ruggish, who had disappeared. Dance Chameleon saw me looking around and whisper-screamed into my ear, "*Denga Wolof?*"

"*Non, mais je parle Français.*" I saw his expression reflect slight disappointment before he smiled again. "*Je m'appele Moise. Et toi?*"

"Jo-Issa," I said, introducing myself.

We continued to dance in silence as DMX's "Ruff Ryders" came on and we both started singing along. He whisper-screamed again, "I love the way you dance."

A man after my heart. "Thank you!"

He continued, "You remind me of Missy Elliott." I tried not to stop dancing and restrained myself from showing offense. I'm sure he meant it as a compliment, but he immediately made me think my "sleek, sexy dance moves" instead looked like large, bouncy hops. In a move that sparked my déjà vu, he asked if I wanted to go outside. I looked around and made eye contact with my cousins to tell them where I was going.

Outside, he introduced me to some of his friends, all of whom were dressed in FUBU, Rocawear, Enyce, and Phat Farm—all the cool brands my mother refused to buy us at home. One of his friends, Kader, was the tall Thuggish-Ruggish I had been eyeing earlier. As we grew closer, Moise would later reveal to me that he thought I was looking at him the entire time; I never denied it. Kader and I shook hands, for far too long, as I realized that I was far too nice to ditch Moise now.

The summer I fell back in love with Senegal is also the summer when I fell in love for the first time. I wasn't looking for Moise, or even checking for him initially, but it was through him that I reenvisioned my heritage through eyes I'd never opened before. He gave me my first uninhibited Dakar experience and taught me so much about what it meant to be Senegalese. I returned to Los Angeles with a new appreciation for who I was and from where I had come. I felt culturally validated and significant in a whole new, confident way. That summer made me realize why my parents, and my mother especially, made sure to abide by the customs and traditions that my father had introduced to her. And I was certain that I would do the same for my children and the children who come after me.

My parents were absolutely pleased with my new appreciation for my family and my country, until they discovered that I had run up our international phone bill by over one thousand dollars in just a month. If only I had had the good sense to develop a program akin to Skype. Maybe dad was right and a computer science degree would have come in handy.

# Fashion Deficient

Some lack common sense; my grandfather lacked two of his five senses, taste and smell; and I lack fashion sense. One needn't feel sorry for me. I was born this way, so it's not as if I knew what I was missing. My ailment was pointed out to me by others, some of whom dropped subtle hints; still others were too disgusted to even bother. I was never fazed by it until my social life was affected.

For a brief period in middle school, T.J.Maxx saved me from complete pariahdom. The day my mother took my younger brother and me there to buy spring clothes, I thought I had found a secret, designer loophole for how I might improve a certain look. "Do people know about this place?" I wondered aloud. It was a stupid question, considering the hangers and marked-down clothes left in disarray everywhere around the store. Tons of people knew about T.J.Maxx, but none were as grateful for it as I.

My introduction to the Los Angeles fashion scene wasn't friendly, by any means. Within the first few weeks of moving from

Maryland and meeting my first L.A. friend, Ashley, I committed my first fashion faux pas, and it was a dangerous one. My idea of good fashion was "matching." If my shirt matched my bottoms, and I had a hair scrunchy and maybe shoes that all matched in some way, I was obviously killing the game. In my younger days, if my average outfit was a paint-by-numbers game, it would consist of one to two numbers, maximum. Solid colors were my best friend. So when Ashley invited me to hang out at her house one crisp summer afternoon, I put on a red shirt, red cotton shorts, red tennis shoes, and a red scrunchy and walked to her home, which stood just on the west side of South Central.

When I knocked on her door, she pulled me in by my arm while she guffawed in her foyer, closing the door behind me.

"What? What's wrong?" I asked, searching her line of sight for the joke.

She pulled herself together enough to point at my torso, tears streaming down her eyes. "Are you crazy?!"

"What do you mean?"

"You're wearing all red in a Crip neighborhood!"

I had absolutely no idea what she was talking about. Word association. Context clues. *Tales from the Crypt. Crypt keepers. Cemeteries. Dead people. Funerals.* Was my outfit somehow disrespecting the dead in some L.A. way? I didn't ask. She was already laughing at my expense and I didn't want to give her more fodder.

I shrugged. "So?"

Her eyes widened, incredulous, "*So?! So?* You want to get shot?"

"If they want to shoot me because I happen to like the color red, then so be it."

Ashley's laughter now turned to concern. It was the kind of

look you give a puppy missing one leg, or a homeless child begging on the street. I didn't know it then, but though she felt sorry for me, she didn't think I was entirely hopeless until the school year started.

Palms Middle School taught me how important name brands were to young black kids who didn't even have an income, much less enough money to afford designer clothes themselves. But in the mid-nineties, Tommy Hilfiger, Ralph Lauren, Nautica, Phat Farm, Donna Karan, K-Swiss, The Gap, Jordans, Sanrio . . . these names held the key to high status and I wasn't acquainted with any of them.

I learned quickly, when one of the many boys I had a crush on started making fun of me for reasons I can't remember. When egged on by one of his friends to "check her tag, check her tag," he reached behind my neck, pulled the tag from my youthful blouse, and chuckled with superiority. "It's not even name brand," he announced, at which point the kids in my class laughed.

Ashley and I didn't have any classes together, but she was very much aware that her help was needed. She wasn't very subtle in offering fashion advice. It started out rather intimately: "You need to start wearing bras."

I was eleven, and my mother had bought me a training bra. I didn't think I needed to wear it, because I was overweight and my "breasts" weren't noticeable and were only the slightest bit convex. But clearly, they were more present than I had assumed. Then, on a bus ride back home from school, she paid me a half compliment. "You should wear more shirts like that, but not as old-lady looking." The shirt I was wearing was accidentally midriff-y, and it belonged to my mother. My mother's closet was massive and she had tons of clothes that back then didn't appeal to me, but came in handy when I was desperate for something to wear. My mother's fashion sense was impeccable. She would consistently receive compliments for some element of her ensemble at every outing. I never really paid attention to this fact, and was only reminded of it whenever my mother would have to insist to me that she knew better about what I should wear than I did.

My mother was particularly invested in my lack of fashion sense, emotionally so. When I was born, the first girl after two boys, my mother was delighted. She would finally get to dress her daughter in cute little dresses and wrap her hair in pretty little bows. Except that due to growing up around boys, I started taking on their traits and coveting their toys and clothes and games, until soon enough, I was repulsed by dresses and bows. My mother tried her best to force me into cute clothes as long as she could, but she could put up with my resistance for only so long. I was a certified tomboy, and she could only hope and pray that I'd grow out of this phase.

I never did. In fact, as her first girl, she was disappointed and even disgusted that I never wanted a sweet sixteen, or to go to the semi-formal or even prom, and that my senior pictures— pictures that were supposed to serve as aesthetically pleasing visual announcements of my transition to adulthood—were a disaster. I got my senior cap-and-gown pictures in the mail and hated them immediately. I went to show my mother, hoping for some empathy or sympathy at the very least, and I was met with antipathy, "What did you expect? You don't even *try*!"

While Los Angeles was successful in making me "name brand" 'are on a small scale, my move to Palo Alto for college cleansed of my materialistic burden. Being among other broke college nts meant I didn't have to care about name brands, because v else did. The illusion was over and my designer shackles eased. It was such a relief!

gh within months, when the weekend "black" parties

would hit, I'd still feel terribly underdressed. Some of these girls were making Ross and Rainbow work for them. Showing up to a party in sweats and a Stanford T-shirt, while acceptable for athletes, was not for a regular black girl who claimed to be from L.A. I befriended a group of girls—Megan, Akilah, and Desiree—who took their wardrobe quite seriously. They were always very complimentary of one another, too.

"Ooo, girl, you look cute!"

"Thanks, girl. I'm loving that top."

"Thanks! I'm stealing those *shoes*."

Then an awkward nod of acknowledgment as they laid eyes on my outfit, and a quick subject change. "Y'all ready to go?"

Don't get me wrong: on the rare occasion that they could compliment any element of my outfit (accessories included), they were more than willing to, but I didn't give them much opportunity. And whenever we'd go out, either collectively or one-on-one, it was pretty clear that I was the "confidence booster" friend, the one girl in the group that you look at and think, "Well, at least I look better than her." There's one in every group and during my first two years in college, I didn't care enough to shed that title. Worrying about what clothes I was going to wear to class and what outfit to wear to a party that featured the same people I had seen on campus earlier in the day was a stress I wasn't willing to take on. In my later years, after returning from a brief Stanford hiatus with my braces shed and money from a job I'd had, I decided I could afford to have a "fresh start" and give my appearance a bit more of an effort. You would have thought I'd removed a goiter from my throat the way the compliments rolled in. "Jo-Issa, you look great!" "Wow, L.A. did you good." "Thank God you're not wearing those stupid-ass Stanford sweats anymore."

Despite the positive affirmations, I still never appreciated fashion as an art form and means of expression until post-college, when I was influenced by three personal and cultural shifts that simultaneously prompted me to reexamine my own sad closet: my move to New York, the release of the movie *The Devil Wears Prada*, and "Umbrella," which marked the beginning of Rihanna's fashion reign. In New York, during my most secluded time period, I was surrounded by the fashionably inclined, and I did not fit in. When I'd be forced to go out at night, or even when I visited my friends Desiree and Kisha in D.C., I was forced to reevaluate my hoodies and jeans and take stock of who I was. At twenty-three, I was a woman, and I needed to start dressing like one. When you're searching for a job or asking people to take you seriously in any capacity, clothes really do matter—and I had to learn that the hard way via failed job interviews and audition rejections.

So then came my discovery of H&M, which was the first shopping experience that didn't exhaust or frustrate me. Since childhood, I've absolutely abhorred shopping. I'm the type to go shopping only when I have a same-day event or if I have a specific singular outfit in mind. Even now, with the convenience of online shopping, I grow overwhelmed by the number of choices available. H&M, filled with "womanly youthful" selections, helped my transition into general fashion appreciation, and the change was noticed by many of my friends and appreciated by my mother when I came home to visit. "Look at you, where did you find that?" she'd ask, with raised brows and a tone of approval.

"In New York," I'd respond casually.

Now, I've regressed. My Awkward Black Girl persona has allowed me an excuse to not "fit in," and I've taken that out and run with it. T-shirts, jeans, and Chuck Taylors are my uniform of choice, and only when necessary (public events, photo shoots, or social gatherings) will I put in the extra effort to "dress up." I admire fashion from a distance and I really do have an appreciation, layered with envy, of those men and women who dress up every day of the week. It just seems so exhausting, but to each his own; if the shoe fits, flaunt it.

Only recently, in an intervention by my publicist and stylist, have I been forced to again take stock of my age and "grow up" where style is concerned. Part of it is my weight gain—skinny people always look great in everything, but when you have an apple-shaped body, loose blouses and tees are *so* much better for the self-esteem. And so I've resolved that the last year of my twenties will be spent getting to a size that makes me comfortable enough to take bold fashion risks. But be warned: should I attain my coveted six-pack, I will never feel obligated to wear *any* clothes. So there.

# New York, NY

It was the second week of June and the summer was off to a promising start. I emerged from the C train on 155th and St. Nick, excited about tomorrow's meeting with a successful television producer. I was going to pitch my college web series, *Dorm Diaries*, with the hopes of turning it into a television show on BET or MTV. I had been sharpening my pitch package *all* week (as opposed to doing the work I was being paid to do), ridiculously excited about what I thought to be a rare opportunity. Having been in New York for less than a year, fresh from college, I was determined to "make it there." Since I had arrived, I was working two jobs and had founded a nonprofit organization called the Black Film Academy, a short-film collective comprised of filmmakers of color determined to reform the image of black film. I had, with the help of my reluctant father, invested in ten thousand dollars' worth of film and editing equipment and, three months prior, we had hosted a successful fund-raising benefit with more than three hundred attendees. Things were moving. Finally, I was on the right track. As

I continued on my path home, I had no idea that my life was about to derail.

The sun was shining, the rats were in hiding, and just as I neared my Washington Heights apartment building, I saw my roommate, Kiki, walking toward our building at the same time. "Roomieboo! Heyyyyyy!" (Roommate + Boo = Roomieboo.) In our near year of living together, we had *never* gotten home at the same time. She was working toward her Master's in Public Health at Columbia and would generally leave early in the morning, while I was working toward figuring out my life at a small not-for-profit theater company in the late afternoon. We were happy as hell to see each other, as if we were old friends reuniting after years and not just a twenty-four-hour lapse. As we talked about our respective days, we were thankful to note that the elevator was working and that we didn't have to walk up five flights of stairs.

The antique elevator doors opened and we hit a left down our dimly lit hallway as I reached for the keys to unlock our apartment. Meanwhile, Kiki continued to discuss our potential plans for the weekend. I inserted the keys, pushed open the door, and was briefly confused to find that the chain on our door was locked from the inside. "What the . . . ?"

Then it clicked. "OH MY GOD!!!" I banged my shoulder into the door in a panic as Kiki looked at me, alarmed and confused. "What? What's happening?"

"The chain! It's locked from the inside! Someone was inside our apartment!" I said, with shrill panic as I banged my body again to try to snap the lock. Successful at last, I dashed inside with Kiki trailing behind me, still registering what I'd just told her. I ran to my room and immediately collapsed internally at what I saw. "No, no, no, no, no, *NO!*" My room had been ransacked. My new Mac laptop, my college PC, all chargers, my brand-new Canon digital film camera and the tripod it sat on, original tapes from a feature film I had been hired to edit—all were gone. "Why the FUCK did they take the tapes?! Those weren't even mine!" That hurt the most, that I was going to have to explain to the filmmaker that the master footage of the film that had taken two years to shoot in Jamaica had been stolen. Who steals mini DV tapes? Days later, when I would tell the story to a friend, she speculated, "Maybe the robbers thought they were sex tapes. You had a camera and tripod set up next to your bed . . ." But I didn't have time to think about all that. Instead, I collapsed on my bed crying. Feeling violated, I reflected on all the memories I'd lost, all the work I had on my computer. My films, my years of pictures, my pitch! All was lost. My life.

Kiki and I sat in the living room, waiting for the police to come, distraught. She, too, had two computers, a digital camera, and a ring. By the time the police arrived, they were pretty useless, and it became very clear to me that they wouldn't be much help. We would have to be our own detectives. First, we started snooping around the building, asking our resident-thug neighbors if they knew anything. They tried to be as helpful as they could, without snitching. Then, we caught a break. One of our neighbors found a bag of clothes and odds and ends and asked if it belonged to us. As we rummaged through the items, Kiki found her digital camera. She scrolled through the pictures and to our surprise, the dumb-fuck robbers had taken pictures of themselves! A set of teenage girls and guys had been squatting in the empty apartment next door and had been watching us. They snuck through my back window via the fire escape and did what they did.

We immediately called the police and showed them the evidence, relieved that we could finally capture these idiotic amateurs and possibly get our stuff back. But their response was almost as bad as the crime itself: "Since they're minors, we can't really do anything about it."

So began a gloomy period. I sent the television producer a somber email asking if we could reschedule the meeting, as all my scripts were on my computers. Of course, I hadn't backed it up. Of course, I didn't have production insurance. These were all hindsight thoughts and I *hated* hearing, "*Well why didn't you just . . .*" or "*You should've . . .*" Why don't people understand that *nobody* wants to hear what they should have done when something has already happened? Don't they know the only question repeating in your head, nonstop, is *what you could have done differently*?

We moved to South Harlem a month later. I put the Black Film Academy on hold indefinitely and continued to work my two jobs. I had already asked my dad for help in buying the film equipment in the first place; I couldn't now ask him to help me to buy a whole new computer. Up until that point, I had only two credit cards activated. Both were maxed out. The third credit card, an American Express with a Stanford Athletics logo, sat in my drawer with the sticker intact. I'd received it in the mail my junior year after a Stanford vs. Berkeley game. There was a sign offering a free Stanford football shirt at a booth, and upon arrival we found out that all we had to do was sign up for a credit card to get the free shirt. "You totally don't even have to use the credit card," the woman said as she dangled a medium-sized shirt before me. I took the credit card out of the drawer, resolving that I was in a state of emergency.

As my debt started to rise and my motivation started to plummet, I found myself writing in my journal one afternoon, sitting on my bed, wondering what I was doing in New York. I loved the city; I loved what it represented. But what was I doing here? Too shy to meet people, I barely went out. I worked *all* the time, at a job that didn't offer any opportunities to move up. Who was I and what did I want to do with my life? I started studying for the LSAT, because maybe my dad was right about going to grad school and having a backup plan. Maybe I got robbed of all my equipment because it was a sign that I wasn't supposed to be pursuing this right now. If I wasn't built for this, not-for-profit work, what was I built for? And suddenly, it hit me: "I'm awkward. And black." One of them I already knew, but the other I had just discovered. It was like a frustrated student discovering she had dyslexia. "I'm not stupid. I just have a learning difference!"

It all made sense: my shyness, all the times I was dismissed for not being "black enough," my desire to reframe the images of black film and television, which I started to do when I created a series in college called *Dorm Diaries*, my inability to dance—these were all symptoms of my Awkward Blackness. *This is an identity*, I thought. I could make T-shirts. I could make sketches/commercials for the T-shirts. Ooh, and what if they were animated? Without knowing it, I started penning an outline of what would be my first and second episodes of *Misadventures of Awkward Black Girl*. I grew excited. *This* was my purpose. This particular moment of despair had sparked my creativity.

But then my heart sank. I was still broke as hell. So I sat on the idea, making a promise to myself to make it happen one day.

The following summer, I flew to Los Angeles for my cousin's graduation. While I was there, I visited two friends from college. One was in film school and the other had just landed a job in the mail room at Creative Artists Agency. We sat on the beach, updating one another on our lives. Then one of my friends turned to me and asked, "Jo-Issa, why are you *still* in New York?"

"What do you mean?" I asked.

"You got robbed. You're broke. It's like you're willingly strug-gling for *no reason*," she continued. "Everybody you know is in Los Angeles. You should just come here. We could do so much together."

I thought about it for a minute. "I can't just get up and leave."

They laughed. "Why not?"

The question haunted me. What was really keeping me there? It wasn't like I had a husband and kids I was tied to, or an amazing, high-paying job. Why *was* I still there? I was young; I didn't have to be tied to any one place.

I told them I'd think about it, and I did. On the plane ride back to New York, I had pretty much made up my mind. My roommate, Kiki, had graduated and gotten a job offer in Los Angeles, so she was happy to hear the news.

That July, I moved back to L.A. with plans to take the reins on my life once more. I didn't make it in New York, but hopefully the assets that were stolen from me will help someone else to make it.

# ABG GUIDE:
# When Co-workers Attack

The co-worker is a necessary evil of the workplace. Even if you're an entrepreneur, or the Chief in Charge, collaborating in some fashion with your colleagues is mandatory and in many situations, it can be unbearably dire. I've had some amazing, generous co-workers and I've had some inconsiderate, hope-they-die-before-five-o'clock co-workers. At least one co-worker in a group of many will be an asshole, an idiot, a suck-up, a know-it-all, a lazy mother%$#@&, or all of the above. To distinguish between them, I've provided yet another handy guide for your benefit and social sanity:

**The Asshole:**
Pretty self-explanatory; this person either loves or hates his job— you really can't tell which because you can't stand to be around his negativity long enough to find out. The asshole co-worker typically makes insensitive jokes (and gets upset when you don't laugh

along), constantly looks out for himself, and finds a way to make every task/experience/part of the job negative.

**THE APPROACH**: Awkwards tend to be passive-aggressive, especially when faced with Asshole co-workers. Avoid doing so, as the Asshole will use that against you. The most foolproof way to deal with an Asshole is to kill him . . . with kindness at every turn. If your co-worker brings up something negative, then find the positive. He will get annoyed with you and avoid you at all costs.

## The Idiot:

How did this fool get a damn job in the first place?! Idiots don't know how to do *anything*, they're constantly wasting time asking questions that have already been answered, and they're slowing up the process for everyone involved. This person is dead weight, and you want nothing more than to sink her at the bottom of the ocean. You might be in a position where the Idiot asks you for your help, over and over again. You've been kind enough to oblige in the past, but now you're carrying the load for two, and nobody has time for that.

**THE APPROACH**: Soft-spoken snide jabs may momentarily alleviate your frustration, but they're falling on dumb and stupid ears. You have to play dumber than dumb. Think of the Idiot as the dumb high school bully (no matter how nice your idiotic co-worker may be) that always cheats off your homework. You have to show her the wrong answers so that she can feel the sting of her own idiocy . . . and then move on to the *next* co-worker for help.

## The Suck-Up:

He will literally kiss the ground his superior has tread. You can look down and see the wet lip imprints on your boss's footsteps; it's *that* bad. This co-worker will throw you under and in front of the bus at any opportunity, if it means that the boss will show him an ounce of attention. It's embarrassing to witness, and you wish you could roofie his drink with a dignity pill.

**THE APPROACH:** Don't try to one-up him; you will lose. Instead, attempt to turn your co-worker's suck-ups into a bonding experience with kinder, more rational colleagues. Literally no one likes a Suck-Up, and if he has been promoted at your expense, then chances are, he has treated other co-workers the same way. Turn the Suck-Up's antics into a drinking game at happy hour with your fellow co-workers and laugh it off.

## The Know-It-All:

She can come off as a Suck-Up, but the Know-It-All is her own breed. Should you have a question or a concern, the Know-It-All will find a way to make you feel stupid about it. The Know-It-All prides herself on knowing everything there is to know about the job at hand, which is great because she's never been promoted and will stay at the same position as long as she's on the job. Knowledge for her means immobility. Know-It-Alls are frequently in the IT department and they hate you.

**THE APPROACH:** Don't take it personally. Don't ever act impressed with the information that a Know-It-All graces you with. Keep your responses/questions/concerns curt and to the point. Don't give this person any excuse to give you more information, because it *exhausts* her. Your very existence is a burden, so try to minimize your breathing in her presence.

## The Lazy M%$#@cka:

Not even worth writing complete sentences about. This co-worker rests on his laurels and lets you do the work. If you have a group presentation or anything that requires collaboration, you can always count on him to contribute jack. At least he's consistent.

**THE APPROACH:** You're only going to get out of not working with this person so many times, and if you continue to do all the work in silence, you will explode, which nobody wants. So, you have to address the problem head on. Tell your fucking boss. Snitches get stitches, but if your job has that good insurance, then it may be worthwhile.

---

One of the worst co-workers I've ever had in the history of all the jobs I've held was all of the above and then some. Her name was Rex, she was in her mid-fifties, and she resembled a dreadlocked Sammy Davis Jr. in face and shape (though she was probably even more petite than I recall, topped off by a large bobble-head). She smelled like menthol cigarettes (and had the smoky breath and stained yellowish-gray teeth to confirm), laughed loud and obnoxiously (especially when she thought you were wrong), and loved to know what I was doing at every single moment.

Our desks were positioned so that mine faced the wall, which was a blessing because I would much rather have been faced with cold, empty nothingness than to have had a default view of her. But on the other hand, while her desk also faced the wall perpendicular to mine, all she had to do was simply turn her head to her left to see all the business I was conducting on my computer. Which she did. Frequently.

On my first day of work, she cozied up to me, exhibiting her friendly side.

"What sign are you?" she asked in a nasally Jersey accent.

"I'm a Capricorn."

She squealed, "So am I! We're both Capricorns." She witch-laughed, gleefully. She started off nice enough, but listening to the way she talked to my boss was aggravating. She would frequently talk to him as though he were stupid and she didn't have the time for his inquiries. I would sit at my desk waiting for the day when he'd snap and fire her, leaving her hopelessly jobless, with no references.

The nonprofit theater company for which I worked had only four employees, including our boss. In short, there was no way to avoid or escape my co-worker. Ever. I relished the hour and a half to two hours I had alone in our office before she arrived at work, at her leisure. Though she was supposed to come in at the same time as I did, she had been working with my boss so long that she felt entitled to come in whenever she damn well pleased. When my boss would, on the rare, careful occasion, tell her to come to work on time, she would screech in a shrill outburst, "YOU KNOW I DON'T WAKE UP BEFORE TWELVE!"

She gave Capricorns a horrible name. Not only was she always late, but she was an absolute mess. All the Capricorns I know are impeccably neat, and her workspace frequently looked like a dirty-booted Tasmanian devil had done the Harlem Shake on her desk. She frequently told me news that I had already heard, as she click-ety-clicked her keyboard, scrolling through her Yahoo News home page with the afternoon recap of stale morning news, asking me, "Did you hear about . . ." for every story she came across.

She was aggravatingly stubborn—it was her way or the highway, and she would cover her ears and shout at the top of her lungs, throwing the geriatric equivalent of a temper tantrum if you challenged her. She was incredibly two-faced, yet convinced that everyone loved her.

The pinnacle moment of intolerance for me was when I had come back to New York from a holiday break in Los Angeles on a Sunday, and then on the phone that Monday morning listened to the final living breaths of the aunt after which I was named. Devastated, I called work, sobbing to another employee who assured me that I should stay home. I came in to work the next day, to sympathetic condolences from everyone, even from Rex (though she kept asking me questions that would trigger more tears). The day after that, my mother told me they were going to hold two services for my aunt on separate weekends. One would be held in the Bay Area, for the community of friends and artists that had loved her so, and the other in Los Angeles, for our entire family. I told her that I couldn't afford to go to the Bay Area service. She was saddened, but she understood.

When I went to tell my boss that I'd be attending the funeral in Los Angeles, and would need to take a Friday off, Rex, who stood next to him in his office, asked, "Didn't you just go?"

It took my all not to roundhouse kick her throat and then body slam her pelvis. Instead, I just glared at her, through slit eyes, incredulous. My actual boss, whom I was addressing in the first place, was more understanding, saying, "Sure, do what you need to do."

Beyond that, Rex was a dream killer. She was a dramaturge, a title she flaunted at every opportunity with pride, but had stayed in the same office, at that same desk, in that same tattered leather chair for over twenty-five years—and it was easy to see why. Each time I'd present a new, potentially innovative idea to try to keep the theater company current and afloat, I'd be met with, "Oh, that will never work," or "Pfft! Good luck with that!"

One time, I took the initiative to make an elaborate marketing proposal for the theater. We hadn't been selling tickets and our donations for the previous quarter had fallen short. I worked for a couple of weeks on my off time, researching the history of the theater and the target audience, along with possible venues and ad sponsorships. When I presented the finished product, Rex's exact words to me were, "You just wasted your time." Then came her sharp, ear-piercing laughter that echoed around the room as she transformed into a bat.

My job would have been a nearly perfect opportunity for growth and learning had a crater opened and consumed her while she happened to be tardily dragging her lazy self to work. She sucked so much life out of me. Still, had it not been for her, I might have stayed way past my expiration date in New York.

The best thing about Rex was that she made me realize that I wasn't satisfied with my current status in life. I wasn't necessarily complacent, but I had been too comfortable and too naïve in hoping that things would change.

Sometimes, it's essential to look at your annoying co-worker and find out what it is that's truly bothering you about them. Is the lazy co-worker's apathy a dis to your inner hard worker's sense of ambition? Is the asshole in customer service helping you to realize the negativity in which you're shrouded? If a company is only as good as its weakest employee, then what does that say about you and the job you hold?

For me, as long as Rex was a part of our roster, there was nothing more I could contribute. So severing ties and starting over was a necessary decision that was practically made on my behalf. I left my job, confident that whatever came next, I'd be better off.

Recently, I went back to visit my old job for the first time in four years and saw Rex sitting in that same, tattered chair, grinning her toothy smile.

"I read about you on my Yahoo News home page. Good for you."

I nodded and smiled. "It's all thanks to you."

The young co-worker who sat in the chair I used to sit in turned around, taking her headphones out of her ears, and smiled at me. I looked at her computer screen, covered with a tinted glare protector. She would be just fine.

# Acknowledgments

I wrote my first book! None of this could have happened without the amazing help and support of these people I'm about to name. I have a huge fear of forgetting to mention important people along the way, so if you don't see your name, it just means that I'm a forgetful, remorseful idiot OR that you just didn't do shit—for the former, I am truly sorry and I will make it up to you.

I have to acknowledge my family first, because they are my absolute everything —and so much of their business is in this book, so they deserve at least that. I'd like to thank my mother, Delyna, and my father, Abdoulaye, for bringing me into the world and encouraging me to give my best and do my best, every step of the way. I love you both so much and hope to make you proud. Amadou, Malick, Lamine, and Elize—the Diop 5—the best siblings a girl could ask for. Thank you for the constant laughs and the constant inspiration and for being my comfort zone. Can't wait to grow old with you guys and raise socially uncomfortable nieces and nephews. Lamine, especially, thank you for getting this process all started for me; you lifted a huge burden off my shoulders during a time I was going through too much.

Memée & Papa, the best grandparents. Memée, thank you for encouraging me to write my very first teleplay for CBS' *Cosby*. I wouldn't have followed through without your encouragement. And Papa, thanks for always being so excited about everything I do and for constantly pushing my siblings and me to collaborate. To my Senegalese clan, *je vous aime, et merci pour tout. A bientot.* To the Camara's, the Charbonnet's, the Hayward's—I love you. To Tantie Rae Beans and Rice, I miss you forever.

Louis, I love you so much. Thank you for bearing with me during the stress and for pushing me during my bouts of insecure laziness. Having you in my corner makes me a happier, better person.

I'd like to thank my team at 3ARTS, the awesome Jonathan Berry, Dave Becky—thank you for helping me to think bigger and do bigger. To my UTA agents Jay Gassner and Tim Phillips—thank you. And to my literary agent Richard Abate—you are an absolute *beast*. I don't know how you do it all with such a calm demeanor. You make shit happen. Thank you for introducing me to Dawn Davis, the most amazing editor in the WORLD! Dawn, thank you so much for instilling a much-needed sense of security in me during this process. You've been such a joy to work with, and I can't imagine having gone through this with any other editor. Thank you for your patience and for getting me. Beryl, thank you for your help and your kindness and for dealing with my false deadline promises—I promise I meant well. Thank you to the entire Simon & Schuster and Atria team. I appreciate you putting your weight behind this project. ALA was so much fun! To Melody Guy, though our time together was brief, I also appreciate you and your work along the way—thank you so much for making this book a possibility and a reality!

To my IRP team—Benoni, Vanessa, Deniese, Candis, Shandrea, Chanda, and my awesome team of interns—thank you for making my professional life such a blast. Each of you guys are amazing and the most ambitious, most thorough people I know. I'm so thankful to have you on my team. Thank your for dealing with all my complaining. You guys are the best.

To my loving family of friends, my vent buddies, my happy places, my motivators, my loves. My Bengali Bestie, Suzanne. My ride-or-die Doublemint Twins—Devin, Daisy, and Jerome. My K/D fam: Mo, Chris, Ashley, Friyana, Damon. To my Stanford Sisters and Girlfriends—Megan and Akilah, Desiree, Adia, Kisha, Kiyana, Maisha. My StanBro's—BJ and Devon. My Bitchiopians: Andunett and Abenet. My Homie Cuz, Theo, and my girl/participant in every endeavor I take on, Leslie.

To my ABG crew—Andrew, Suj, Tristen, Lyman, Leah, Hanna, Tracy, Madison, Michael, Shea, Isaac, Duran, Marissa, Isaac, Eric, Ecuadorian Jorge, Puerto Rican Jorge, Travis—thank you all for being so down for the cause and for making ABG what it is. To Pharrell, Mimi, Caron, and Robin—thank you for taking Awkward Black Girl to the next level and for being such a positive, welcoming team.

To the amazing teachers and mentors I've had over the years, who have encouraged me and instilled confidence in my writing and pushed my creativity: Mr. Freedman, Ms. Thigpen, Ms. Fletcher, Ms. Golden, Ms. Guy, Ms. Ellis, Mr. Segal, Professor Harry Elam, Professor Michele Elam, Jan Barker Alexander, Carolus Brown, Professor Diggs.

To Shonda Rhimes, Betsy Beers, Rachel Eggebeen, Allison Eakle—thanks for being the best creative team I've ever worked with. Thank you for taking a chance and for your patience, and for putting me on the radar of many. You guys are killing the game and SO inspirational.

To Larry Wilmore, you are a dream. I will miss you. But you'll never get rid of me. Thank you for being so positive and so funny and so awesome and so humble and such a damn boss.

To Seth Brundle the stylist, Kamaren Williams the make-up artist, and Felicia Leatherwood the natural hair guru—thank you for making me look glamorous on my very first book cover!

Thank you to all my supporters, Twitter friends, Facebook friends, Instagram friends, anybody who has ever written an encouraging word, shared my work, or donated money or time to helping me make things happen. I really truly appreciate you and none of this could have happened without you.

# About the Author

With her own unique flair and infectious sense of humor, Issa Rae's content has garnered more than 20 million views and 200,000 subscribers on YouTube. In addition to making *Glamour* magazine's "35 Under 35" list (2013) as well as Forbes's "30 Under 30" list (2013 and 2014) and winning the 2012 Shorty Award for Best Web Show for her hit series *The Misadventures of Awkward Black Girl*, Issa Rae has worked on web content for Pharrell Williams, Tracey Edmonds, and more. Issa has received national attention from major media outlets including *The New York Times*, CNN, MSNBC, *ELLE*, *Seventeen*, *Rolling Stone*, *VIBE*, *Fast Company*, *Essence*, *FADER*, and more. Issa is represented by 3ARTS Entertainment.

Get email updates on

# ISSA RAE,

exclusive offers,

and other great book recommendations

from Simon & Schuster.

———————————

Visit **newsletters.simonandschuster.com**

or

scan below to sign up: